Shreveport's Historic Oakland Cemetery

Spirits of Pioneers and Heroes

Gary D. Joiner, PhD & Cheryl White, PhD

The History Press

Published by The History Press
Charleston, SC 29403
www.historypress.net

Front cover, bottom: Courtesy of Cheryl H. White.
Back cover: Courtesy of Gary D. Joiner.
First published 2015

Manufactured in the United States

ISBN 978.1.62619.838.8

Library of Congress Control Number: 2014958801

This book is dedicated to those who lost their lives in the great yellow fever epidemic of 1873 in Shreveport

Contents

Contents

Acknowledgements

There are several people who have contributed to make this work possible. The authors would like to acknowledge the research assistance of our students at Louisiana State University–Shreveport, especially Lela Robichaux and Angel Smith, as well as Abby Patton Genka, who generously allowed us to photograph her family's Howard Association "Angel of the Epidemic" medal from the great yellow fever epidemic of 1873. In addition, we are indebted to the Noel Archives at LSU–Shreveport, Caddo Parish registrar of voters Ernie Roberson, *Shreveport Times* reporter John Andrew Prime and, of course, the pioneering work of Shreveport historian Eric Brock, who passed away in 2011 and now rests eternally in this beautiful cemetery. Lastly, we would like to thank the Oakland Cemetery Preservation Society (OCPS), whose members tirelessly work to maintain and preserve Shreveport's most important historic landmark.

Introduction

Oakland Cemetery

There may not be a more picturesque and peaceful spot in all of Shreveport than the historic Oakland Cemetery. It is a veritable "who's who" of Shreveport history, for walking among its markers reveals much about the past. Recorded burials began elsewhere in Shreveport in 1840, even though the city did not officially establish Oakland Cemetery until 1847. By mayoral decree that year, Lawrence Pike Crain required that all bodies buried within Shreveport should be placed in Oakland Cemetery: "Whereas the Mayor and Trustees of the town of Shreveport have purchased the ten acre lot known as Number Eighteen for a burial ground for the said town: 1) all persons buried in corporation limits shall be buried in said burial ground."[1] As a result, some bodies buried prior to this time were moved.[2] The oldest burial in Oakland, by visual inspection, appears to be that of Rufus Sewall, the second mayor of Shreveport, who was killed in a duel in 1842. The city sold burial plots in Oakland until 1930.[3] The last burial to take place in the cemetery was in 2011, when, by special arrangement, the city permitted the burial of Shreveport historian Eric Brock. It is an unfortunate footnote that today, the cemetery continues to be the victim of both neglect and malicious property damage, although dedicated preservationists work diligently to maintain this remarkable reminder of the past. The Oakland Cemetery Preservation Society, in partnership with the City of Shreveport, has made great strides in stabilizing, researching, mapping and preserving this historic landscape.

The same mayoral decree that created Oakland Cemetery required that it be divided into three sections: one for the creation of a "potters field," one to be set aside for mayors and trustees, and one to be sold to private individuals. The city created the position of cemetery sexton for the ongoing care and maintenance of the burial grounds, stipulating also that until the area could be properly surveyed, all burials had to be performed in the southeast section.[4] This explains why many of the earliest graves are concentrated in this section.

For Shreveport, this sacred ground continues to represent a history classroom of sorts, eternally imprinted with the lives of the city's past. Dates and names carved in stone are much more than simple markers of lives that once were; they are also living memorials of Shreveport history. So many of those who lie in Oakland Cemetery could be a chapter of their own in the great story of the city so significant were their contributions to the unique flavor and allure of the city by the Red River. Notably, Oakland Cemetery is the final resting place for around eight hundred victims of the city's yellow fever epidemic of 1873.[5] The death toll mounted so rapidly during that fateful summer that city officials did not have time to arrange for timely proper burials. A mass grave is now marked with a simple monument, but it remains one of the most visited sites in the cemetery.

There is also significant cultural history told among the graves at Oakland. Jews escaping the anti-Semitism of Europe in the early nineteenth century came in large numbers to the South, and many settled in and around the booming Shreveport area. The Hebrew Mutual Benevolent Association purchased a tract of ground within Oakland in 1859 that became the first burial place for Jews within the city.[6] This one-acre plot is a poignant reminder even today of the numbers of Jews who sought new lives and refuge in this part of the world during times of great persecution.

Oakland Cemetery is the final resting place for mayors, Confederate veterans (and some Union soldiers), prominent early citizens and even the famous "Shreveport Madam," Annie McCune. Bankers, lawyers, judges and politicians can be counted among the dead resting here. In some cases, family plots contain the remains of numerous members of the same influential family, as with James Martin Foster and his family. Behind each monument or marker, there is a story that is important to Shreveport's identity. The stories are poignant, inspirational, funny and sometimes tragic, as in the case of the two grandchildren of President Zachary Taylor who are buried in Oakland. There are also those who are known to be buried within the cemetery walls but whose grave spots are unmarked; this work remembers them as well.

This work provides the reader with the opportunity to get to know the past through the stories of these men and women who are sharing eternity together in the beautiful rolling terrain and shady trees of Oakland Cemetery, surely Shreveport's most significant historic landmark.

This Quiet Dust Was Gentlemen and Ladies

This quiet dust was gentlemen and ladies
And lads and girls;
Was laughter and ability and sighing,
And frocks and curls;

This passive place a summer's nimble mansion,
Where bloom and bees
Fulfilled their oriental circuit,
Then ceased like these.

—Emily Dickinson

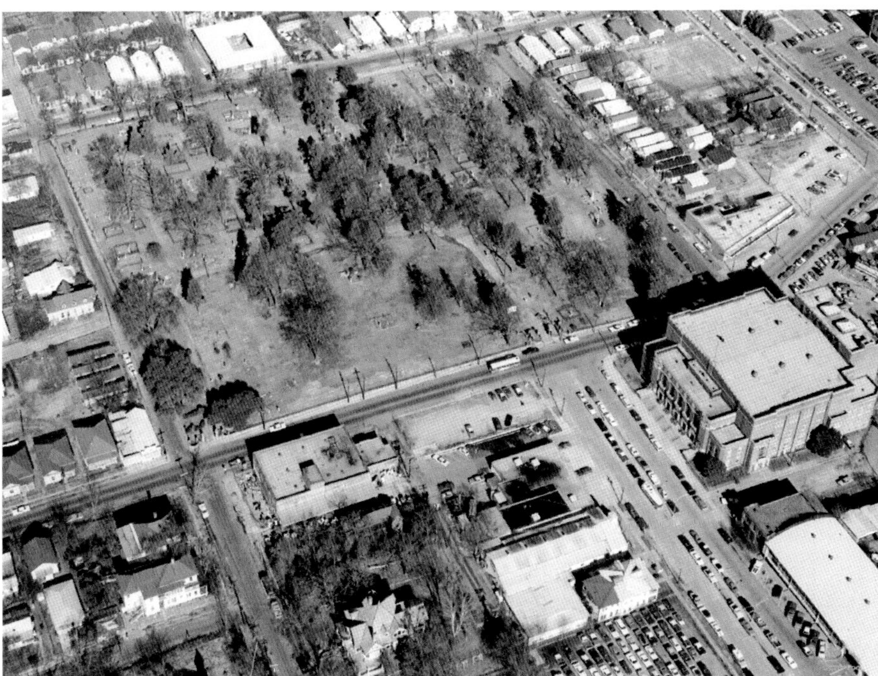

In this aerial photograph of Oakland Cemetery from around 1958, the neighborhood surrounding the cemetery is still vibrant and commercially active. *LSU Shreveport, Noel Memorial Archives.*

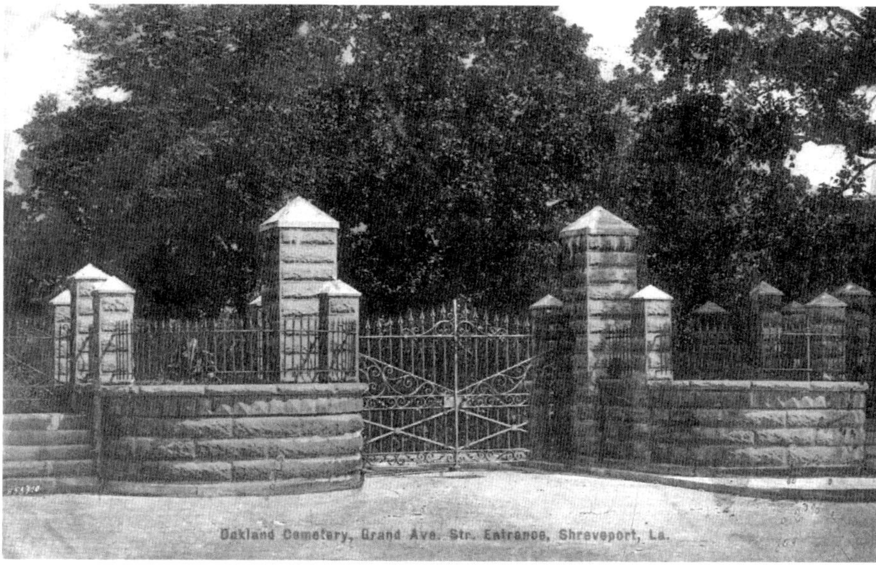

The Grand Avenue (Elvis Presley Boulevard) main gate into Oakland Cemetery from a postcard in 1906. *Collection of Gary D. Joiner.*

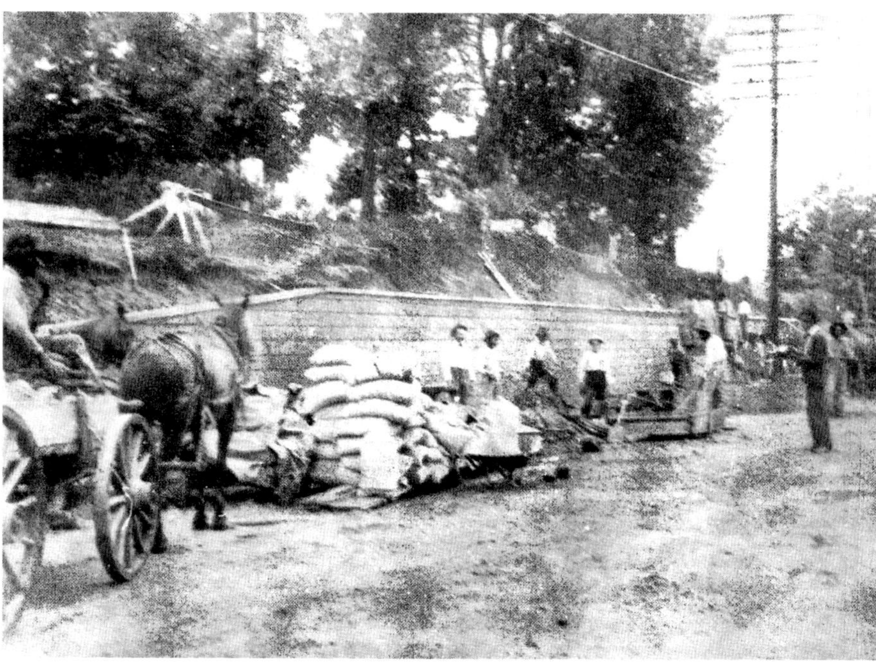

Chatwin brothers' crews build the Christian Street and Sprague Street wall segments of Oakland Cemetery in 1905. *LSU Shreveport, Noel Memorial Archives.*

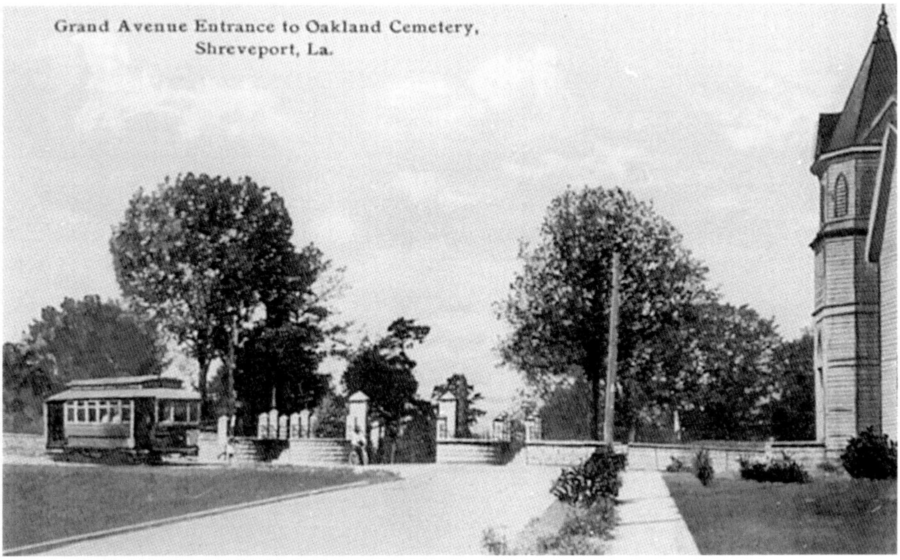

Postcard of the main entrance of Oakland Cemetery from around 1906. *Collection of Gary D. Joiner.*

Alexander John Boarman

This man has the interesting historical distinction of being Shreveport's youngest mayor but oldest federal judge. Nicknamed "Aleck," Alexander John Boarman was a native of Yazoo City, Mississippi, born in 1839, the very year that Shreveport was established. He came to Shreveport as a young child with his parents and, as a young man, left to pursue studies at the University of Kentucky. He returned to Shreveport upon his graduation in 1860 and was interning to study law, but the outbreak of war meant those career plans would be delayed. Boarman entered Confederate service in the esteemed volunteer "Caddo Rifles," mustering into Company A of the 1st Louisiana Regiment on April 28, 1861, and eventually becoming its captain.[7] By the end of the war, he had attained the rank of major in the Army of Northern Virginia and was discharged with an impressive service record.[8]

In 1866, Boarman became mayor of Shreveport and, at the age of twenty-six, was the youngest to serve in that office. At the same time, he was finally admitted to the bar. He enjoyed a career in public service that also included a term on the city council and representing Louisiana's Fourth Congressional District in the U.S. House of Representatives from 1872 to 1873. He also served as judge of the Tenth Judicial District Court in Caddo Parish.[9]

In March 1881, Congress created the U.S. District Court for the Western District of Louisiana, which was composed of forty parishes, and placed the seat at Shreveport. President James Garfield appointed Boarman to the post, and the court met in rooms at 513 Spring Street. The first true federal courthouse was built in 1887 on Texas Street, eventually replaced by the 1911 construction of

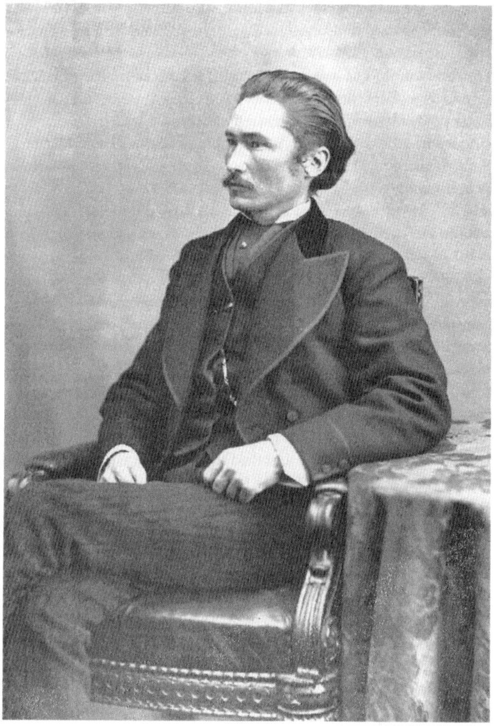

Left: Image of Aleck Boarman as a federal judge. *Courtesy of U.S. First District Court for the Western District of Louisiana.*

Below: Aleck Boarman's ground tablet monument in Oakland Cemetery. *Photograph by Gary D. Joiner.*

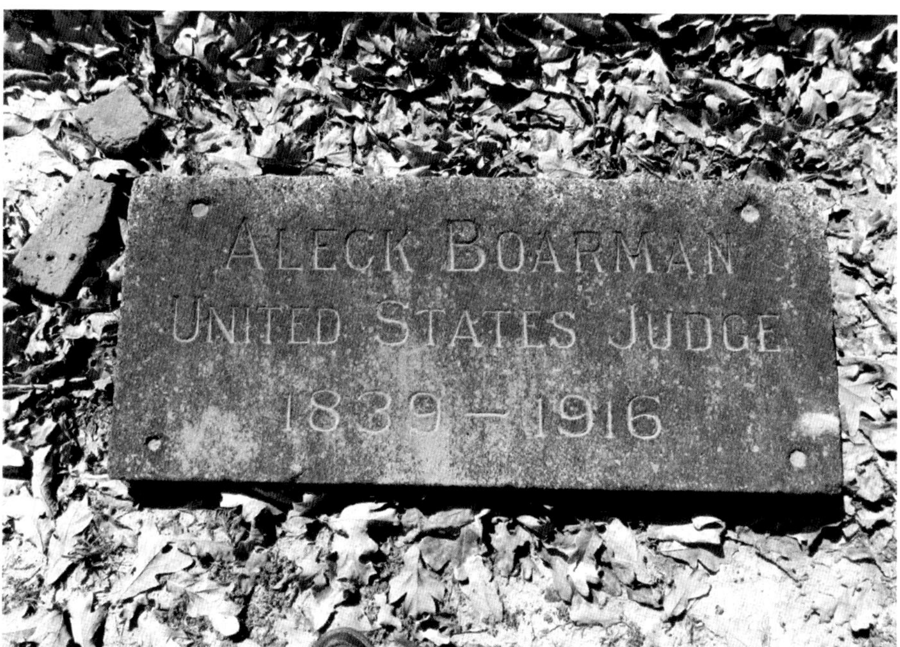

a new federal building currently housing the Shreve Memorial Library.[10] Judge Boarman oversaw the construction of both courthouses, with his tenure as judge lasting until his death in 1916. At age seventy-seven, this made him the oldest-serving federal judge.[11]

Boarman is buried within one of the two Elstner family plots within Oakland Cemetery near his niece Julia Elstner. His final resting place is signaled by a large granite marker that is distinctive in its simplicity. The memorial is inscribed with only his name, dates of birth and death and clearly what was the high point of his career, "United States Judge."

Jacob Bodenheimer

Appearing very early in the story of the settlement of Shreveport was a young German immigrant who braved a journey to the unknown as a very young man. Born in 1808, Jacob Bodenheimer came from Niederhochstadt, Germany, as a teenager, making his way to north Louisiana from New Orleans as early as 1827. Besides probably being the first Jewish settler in the area, he came to this part of Louisiana before either Shreveport or Bossier City existed, settling in Bossier Parish.[12] Jacob was just fourteen years old when he stowed away on a sailing ship, and when he arrived in New Orleans in 1822, it is believed he spoke no English at all. It is difficult to imagine today that a teenager would have had the courage for a journey such as this, to say nothing of the task of building a new life in a completely foreign place at such a young age.

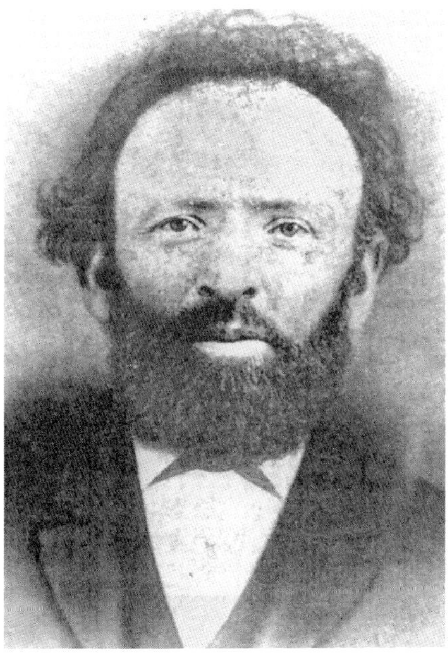

This is the only known image of Jacob Bodenheimer. *Image courtesy of Goldring/Woldenberg Institute of Southern Jewish Life.*

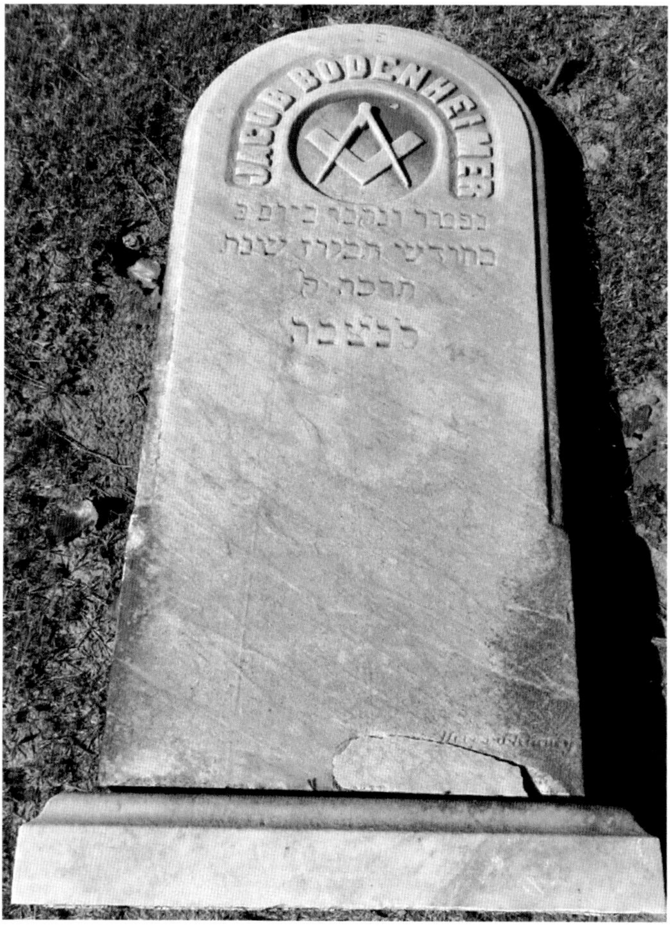

The broken tombstone of Jacob Bodenheimer. *Photograph by Gary D. Joiner.*

Bodenheimer married his wife, Eliza Weil, also a German Jewish immigrant, in New Orleans in 1832. They moved northward in the late 1830s, traveling by keelboat on the mostly obstructed Red River, another daunting undertaking. He reached Loggy Bayou in southern Bossier Parish before losing all his possessions when the boat sank there. Eventually, Bodenheimer was able to establish a home and a living by offering a ferry service on Lake Bistineau, before moving to Bellevue, Louisiana, and building a hotel, livery and general store. The teenage stowaway from Germany became a successful businessman and family man in north Louisiana just as the region was beginning to thrive with settlers and commerce.

One of Bodenheimer's sons, Emmanuel, became the first and only mayor of South Highlands in 1915, before the neighborhood was incorporated into the city of Shreveport in 1927. Another son, Henry, also served in city government and established a successful insurance company in Shreveport. A daughter, Harriette, married Captain Simon Levy in 1866. The Bodenheimer family represented the beginning of a Jewish migration to the area that continued in large numbers until after the Civil War. By 1858, the Hebrew Benevolent Society (which would become the Shreveport Jewish Federation) dedicated the "Hebrew Rest" area of the city's Oakland Cemetery, reflecting the influx of Jewish settlers.[13]

Jacob contracted malaria and died in March 1865. The inscription on his monument reads, "May His Soul Be Placed in the House of the Lord." Following his death, his widow, Eliza, married Jacob Citron in 1867 but divorced him in 1888. All of these Bodenheimers are buried in Hebrew Rest.

Mary Bennett Cane

The most influential woman in the early history of both Shreveport and Bossier City rests eternally in one of the most visited plots of historic Oakland Cemetery. Mary Doal Ciley Bennett Cane, who died in 1902, was the wife of two prominent early pioneers. She was married first to William Smith Bennett, one of Shreve Town's original founders. After Bennett's death in 1837, she married James Huntington Cane, her first husband's partner, with whom she built a majestic home, Elysian Grove, on the Bossier City side of the Red River. Her home there was partially constructed of timber shipped from her native New Hampshire.[14] The influence of Cane is obvious in the earliest names attached to the east side of the river: Cane's Landing and Cane City.[15]

Mary was born in New Hampshire in 1812, purportedly the illegitimate daughter of a gambler, and died nearly ninety years later as one of the wealthiest women in the South.[16] Most of her expansive life was spent in the Shreveport–Bossier City area. As a proprietor and part owner in the Cane and Bennett commercial trading enterprises on both sides of the river, she became quite influential through the use of her wealth and status as a first citizen. It is an interesting twist of history that she is actually buried within the walls of Oakland Cemetery, on land that she donated to the city of Shreveport through a tax swap. Cane also donated the land where Princess Park is located. Her reputation as a patroness of the arts, a generous benefactor of many causes and a true pioneer of what was once western frontier make Mary Bennett Cane a fascinating historical anomaly.

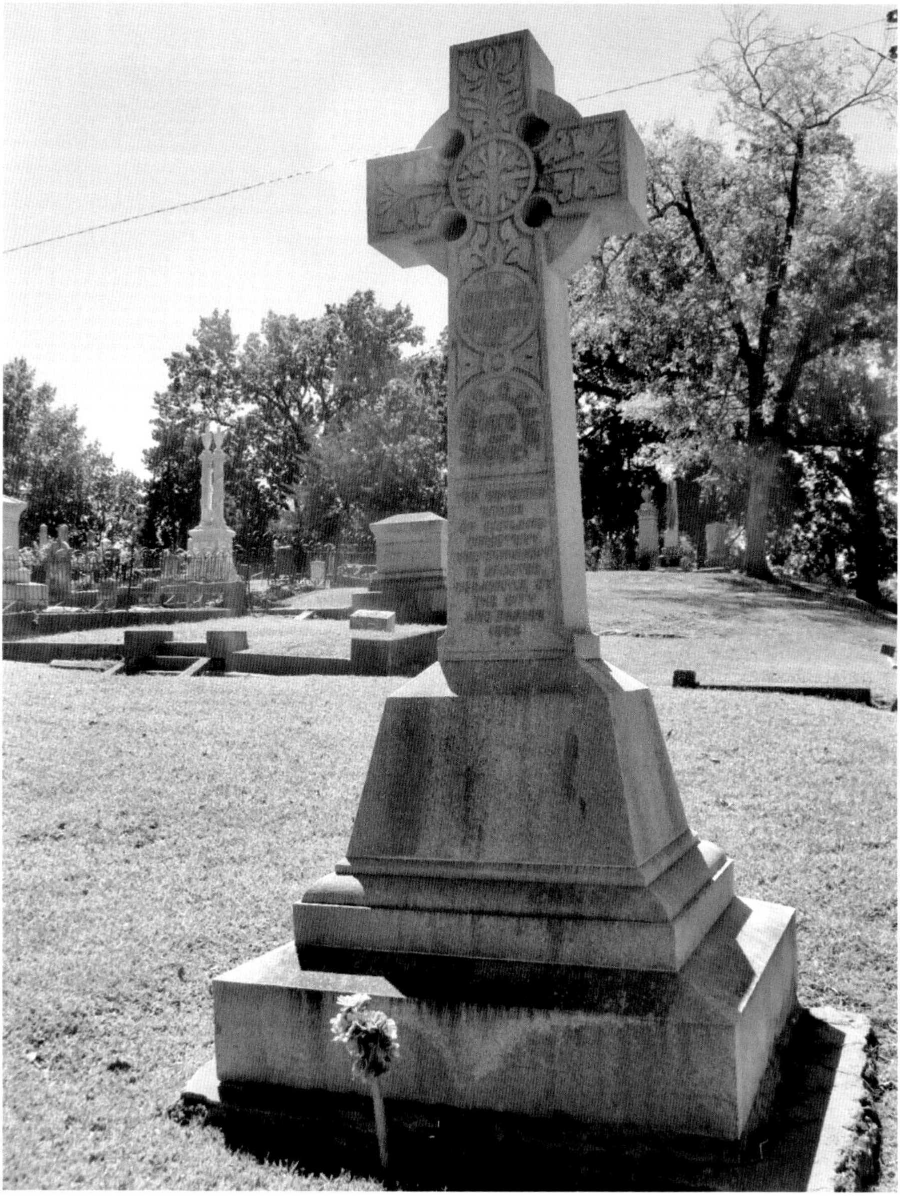

Mary Bennett Cane's magnificent Celtic cross monument is located near the north wall of Oakland Cemetery. *Photograph by Gary D. Joiner.*

When she arrived in the area as a young woman in her twenties, Mary was the wife of William Bennett. Yellow fever claimed Bennett first and then Cane's wife, so in 1839, James Cane and Mary Bennett became more than just accidental business partners. They became man and wife. In a fashion that was quite unusual in the early nineteenth century, Mary worked out the equivalent of a prenuptial agreement with Cane that would allow her to retain her inheritance from Bennett separate from the marital estate. Once again, however, she was to find herself widowed in 1845. James Cane also died of yellow fever. She later married a third time, in 1850, to a riverboat gambler named Granville Alexander, but she sued him for divorce a few years later. It is a testament to her prestige and influence that the divorce was not only granted but that two attempts by her former husband to lay claim to community property were also legally denied.[17]

Mary Bennett Cane gave birth to three children, but only one lived to adulthood, a daughter named Jennie. When Mary died in 1902, the Shreveport City Council voted to erect a monument to her at her grave in Oakland Cemetery. It is a tall Celtic cross, large enough in stature to memorialize the "Mother of Shreveport." William Smith Bennett is believed to be buried in a block adjacent to and north of Oakland Cemetery. There is no evidence of the burial, but an early development map shows the north third of the block listed as "Bennett and Cane Cemetery." On the east side of the block and running near her grave site lies Mary Court, named for her. James Huntington Cane was buried near the riverbank at Elysian Grove. The grave site was washed away in the great flood of 1908.

Amanda Arnell Clark and Dr. Dickerson Alphonse Smith (Mother and Son)

Amanda Arnell Clark was a slave born in St. Joseph, Missouri, in 1840.[18] She moved to Shreveport after receiving her freedom and an inheritance of $1,000 from her former owner, Luther Arnett.[19] She became a noted Shreveport philanthropist and real estate developer. Among the properties she developed were those along Austin Place. Amanda passed that influence on to her son, Dickerson Alphonse Smith. Smith was the first African American physician to practice in Shreveport and the first African American member of the Shreveport Medical Society. He was head of the Shreveport Charity Hospital's "colored wing" and, later, the hospital itself. Interestingly, his life spanned two quite different eras. Late-nineteenth-century restrictions on people of color in the South represented the social norm. However, by the early twentieth century, progress in equality of education and opportunity was becoming evident. Dr. Smith is an example of this progress, being of the first generation born as the institution of American slavery ended.

Clark also used her inheritance to make sure her son received an education and went to medical school. Smith went to Chicago to study at Rusk Medical College, where he graduated in 1892, which was the same year his mother died. He married his wife, Frances, in 1893, and they also made their lives in Shreveport. In keeping with his mother's philanthropic tradition, Dr. Smith established a home for indigent elderly in Cedar Grove in 1930, in addition to maintaining properties his mother built downtown. Part of her original

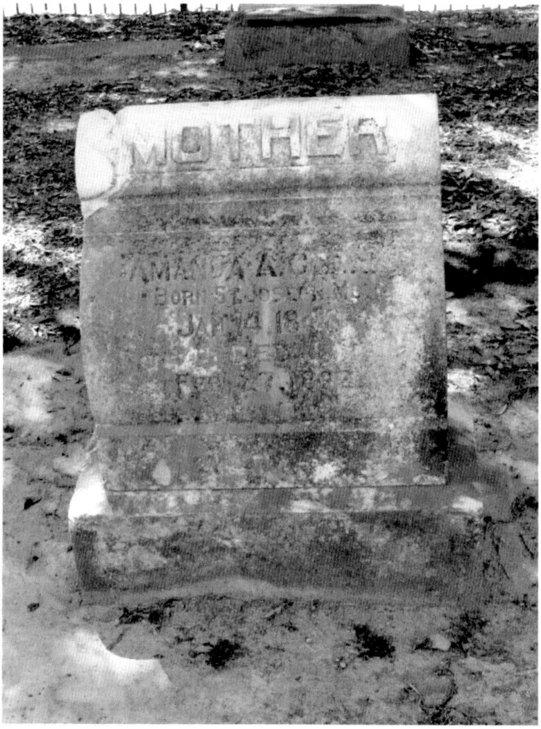

Left: The tombstone of Amanda Clark is located near the western wall of Oakland Cemetery. *Photograph by Gary D. Joiner.*

Below: The tombstone of Dickerson Smith lies directly behind and west of the monument to his mother. *Photograph by Gary D. Joiner.*

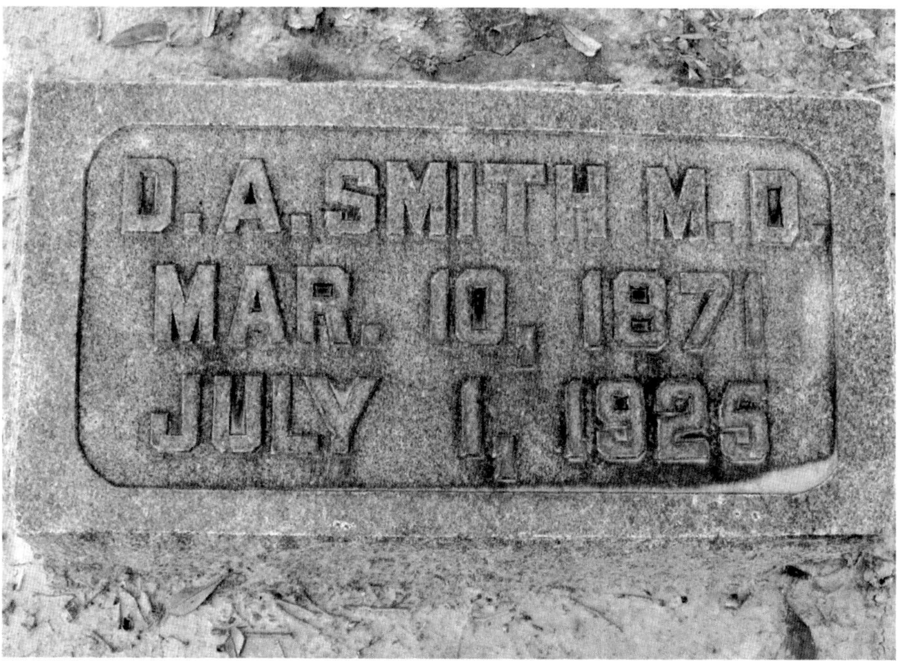

property is now occupied by the old Joe D. Waggoner federal building, and two others still stand at 211 and 215 McNeil Street.[20] Amanda's home was on the west side of McNeil Street at 206. Dr. Smith enjoyed a successful medical career until his death from a cerebral hemorrhage in 1925.

Mother and son Amanda Clark and Dickerson Alphonse Smith are buried near each other in Oakland Cemetery, facing Christian Street (just north of Austin Place).

Lawrence Pike Crain

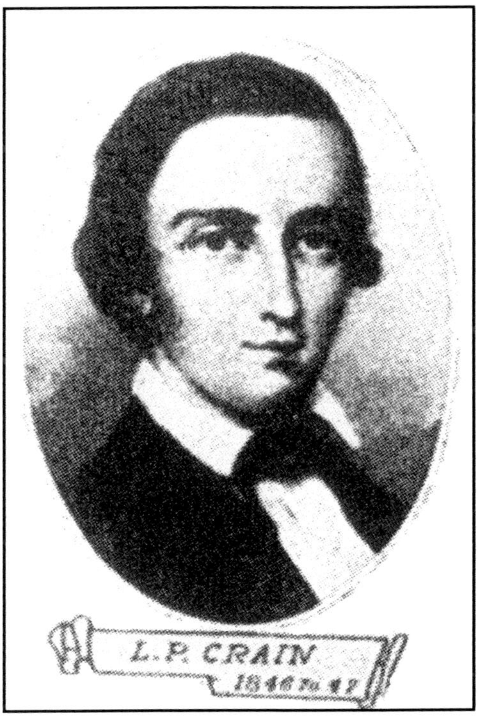

This image of Lawrence Pike Crain is from late in his life. *LSU Shreveport, Noel Memorial Archives.*

One of Shreveport's youngest mayors, Lawrence Pike Crain, has an interesting legacy in the annals of city history. Had his life not suddenly ended at the age of forty-one, Crain is someone who doubtlessly could have contributed much more. A Virginia native who moved with his family to Rapides Parish, Louisiana, while he was still a child, Crain was just twenty-three years old when he was elected to serve on the board of trustees (now Shreveport City Council) in 1841. He was reelected multiple times to the post and served for much of his life until his death. In 1846, Crain became Shreveport mayor, as only the sixth man to have held the office and the second youngest to ever hold that office (he was twenty-

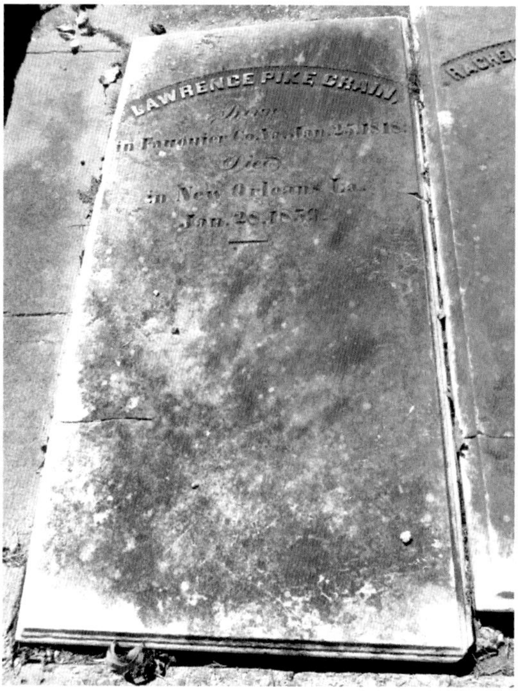

Basal monument of Lawrence Pike Crain is located near the eastern wall of Oakland Cemetery. *Photograph by Gary D. Joiner.*

eight years old when elected). Shreveport was a young city, at one time the farthest point west in the United States, and it is helpful to remember this when considering the anomaly of Crain's public service. It is unusual that Crain continued to occupy the seat of a city councilman even while he simultaneously served as mayor. Of course, such a thing would be unthinkable today.

In 1848, Crain married Rachel Stokes, and the couple had four sons: John, Robert, Montfort and Lawrence Sidney. The Crains' daughter-in-law (married to Lawrence Sidney) was Mary Ford, the daughter of Reverend J. Franklin Ford of the First Presbyterian Church. The Crains were charter members of this early Shreveport religious community, although records indicate they were also involved with the establishment of St. Mark's Episcopal Church in 1851.[21] Their family tale is indicative of how closely related the distinguished families of the area actually were. The family home was located at the corner of Milam and Market Streets and was purported to have been a grand example of New Orleans–style architecture, complete with grand balconies and cast-iron work.[22]

In addition to being mayor at the time of the acquisition of land from Mary Bennett Cane to be set aside for Oakland Cemetery in 1847, Crain helped codify the city ordinances of Shreveport for the first time in 1849. This was a significant step in advancing Shreveport from the status of a frontier town that administered random justice to that of a modern city. Interestingly, Crain's reputation and standing could certainly have placed him on a trajectory to higher office, but Crain repeatedly refused to run because he thought it would cost him friendships.[23]

Crain died in 1859 at the St. Louis Hotel in New Orleans, where he was celebrating his forty-first birthday. He fell suddenly ill and succumbed to tuberculosis just three days later. He rests in Oakland beneath a large gray marble slab next to his wife, four sons, his daughter-in-law and one granddaughter. The large family plot is completely surrounded by stone and accented at the center with a simple marble marker bearing the surname of Crain.

Moses H. Crowell

Moses Crowell was mayor of Shreveport at a colorful and interesting time in the city's history, for it was a period that witnessed three rival claimants to the office following a disputed 1871 election. During the summer of 1871, not only were there three men claiming to be mayor, but there were also two rival city councils in existence! Both councils operated independently, each claiming to be legitimate, with mayoral administrations that paralleled them both. In addition to the challenges of financing rival city governments, even for a brief period of time, there was the confusion that prevailed over which contracts were legal and valid and which city ordinances citizens would be expected to obey. This morass of legal issues was centered on federal control of Shreveport during the depths of Reconstruction. The U.S. Army enforced the will of the Grant administration and Congress. Caught in the middle of local issues across the South, they often played a "wait and see" attitude.

The previous occupant of the mayor's office, Jerome Bonaparte Gilmore, decided to not seek reelection in 1871, leaving two candidates vying for the office—Moses Crowell and William Shivers. Crowell was a Virginia native who achieved the rank of major in the U.S. Army and was commander of a corps of Union troops dispatched to Louisiana as an occupation force. Shivers was a local man who had fought for the Confederacy. Given the Reconstruction politics that prevailed at the time, Crowell was therefore unpopular with some Shreveport citizens, but the election nevertheless proved to be close. The official vote count had Shivers winning, 371 to 347.[24]

However, the Louisiana state legislature passed a bill during the summer of 1871 that permitted the governor to appoint city officials in lieu of elections. This was perhaps an attempt to cool tensions related to federal occupation during Reconstruction, but it meant near chaos for the city. As it turns out, Governor Warmoth's choice for Shreveport mayor was Moses Crowell. The situation was further complicated because the process of reordering city government also left the Gilmore administration intact.

Suit was brought in the Tenth Judicial District Court to resolve the three-mayor dilemma, and in the meantime, William Shivers died. The court held that Warmoth's appointment of Crowell was legal, but Gilmore appealed the decision to the Louisiana State Supreme Court, an action that only resulted in further confusion and delay when that body said the case must be retried.[25] In the end, it was compromise between the factions that brought an end to the divided city government, and Crowell prevailed as mayor. He worked to enhance Shreveport's viability as a rail center but resigned in March 1873, just months before the city was struck by a horrific yellow fever epidemic. He remained in Shreveport until his death in 1875. He is buried under an unmarked grave in Block 8.

Adah Vinson DeLay

The daughter of Shreveport mayor Richard Vinson (profiled separately in this volume), Adah Vinson DeLay became one of the most significant and generous philanthropists in Shreveport history. In 1900, Adah married Cyril DeLay, the editor of the *Shreveport Times*, but she was widowed within two years at the very young age of twenty-two. She used the influence and resources available to her to support a number of causes, including the care of Oakland Cemetery, but especially for her work in caring for and finding homes for orphaned or abandoned children. Although she never had any children of her own, DeLay nevertheless served in the role as mother to hundreds.

In 1912, DeLay took over the management of the children's ward at Charity Hospital (soon to be known as Confederate Memorial). DeLay provided many needed medical items for the ward and also was known to provide funerals for children who died without financial means. She also began a habit of providing a Christmas tree to the ward every year and gifting each child with something from Santa Claus. It was this practice that earned her the beloved nickname of "the Christmas Tree Lady." The generosity of her Christmas tree legacy was widely known and enjoyed, even by city officials.[26]

At the turn of the twentieth century, Shreveport did not have any official adoption agencies or means to care for homeless children. DeLay took it upon herself to remedy this by taking such children into her own home, if necessary, until a permanent home could be found.[27] This is the task to

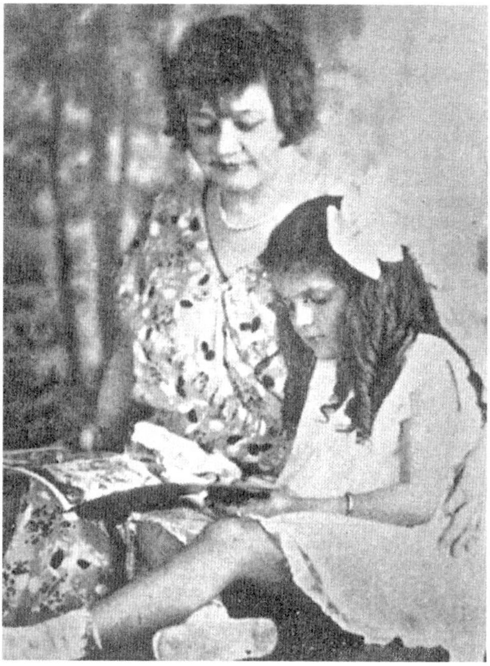

which the young Adah DeLay set herself, laboring tirelessly and at her own expense to act as a social safety net and advocate for hundreds of children. She never remarried, and indeed, she made this the work of her entire lifetime.

Adah Vinson DeLay died in Shreveport in 1933 at the age of sixty, and she is buried in the family plot at Oakland Cemetery along with her parents and her husband. It is perhaps indicative of how much she had depleted her financial resources that she did not have a marker of her own until a fine granite stone was placed on her grave in 1995 by the United Daughters of the Confederacy. Adah DeLay's legacy is represented by the hundreds of children she helped to find permanent and happy adoptive homes.

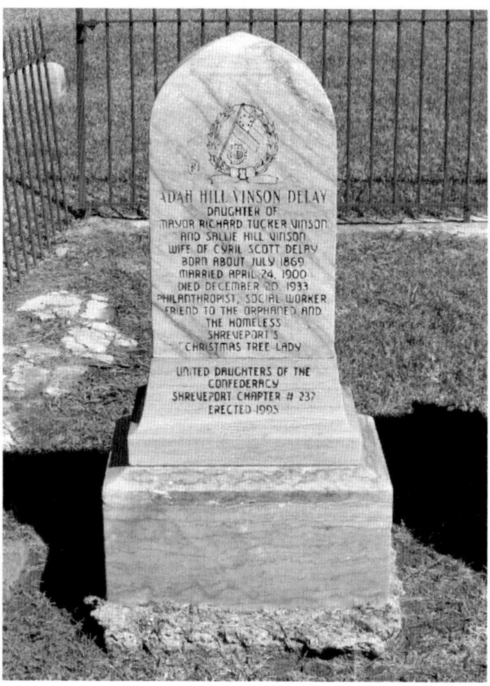

Top: In this photograph of Adah Vinson DeLay, she poses with a child. *Circa 1930 photograph from the* Shreveport Times, *LSU Shreveport, Noel Memorial Archives.*

Left: Adah Vinson DeLay's monument was erected by the United Daughters of the Confederacy. *Photograph by Gary D. Joiner.*

Bartholomew Egan

A native of Killarney, Ireland, and born in 1795, Egan migrated to the United States, received medical training in Virginia and, finally, settled near Mount Lebanon in Bienville Parish in 1847. He was a significant pioneer in the establishment of the antebellum community there. Egan became president of Mount Lebanon University, the first university in north Louisiana. Converting from Roman Catholicism to the Baptist tradition, Egan was the founder of the Louisiana Baptist Convention. By 1863, the Mount Lebanon facility had become primarily a hospital and nursing home for wounded Confederate soldiers and veterans, and the school officially closed for educational purposes that same year. By 1882, the buildings were repurposed to open Mount Lebanon High School but were finally destroyed by fire in 1886.[28] The facility was vitally important to north Louisiana during the war, as was the service of Bartholomew Egan, who became surgeon general of the state of Louisiana.

Egan's leadership during the Civil War led Confederate president Jefferson Davis to remark of him that "he was one of the ripest scholars of his age."[29] His contributions to the city of Shreveport are also etched in the public record. In his official report to General Thomas Manning, adjutant general of Louisiana, dated December 23, 1863, Egan noted, "At Shreveport I was called upon unexpectedly to improvise a hospital, in which one hundred seventy-five patients, many laboring under alarming diseases, were treated."[30] This became part of the Confederate Marine Hospital. It was located in a valley between large hills on what is today Greenwood Cemetery.

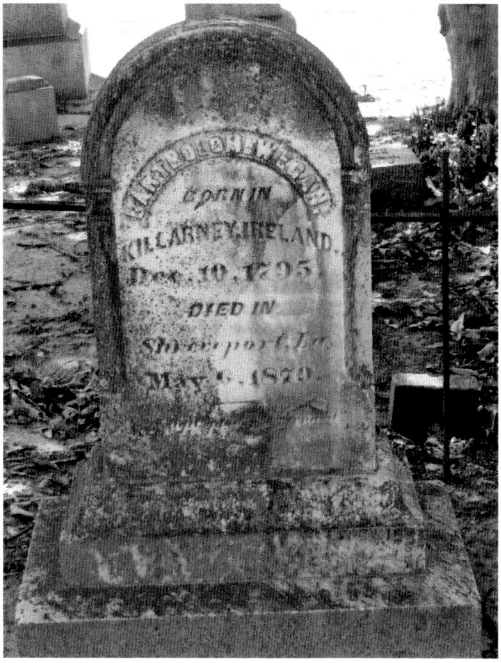

Bartholomew Egan's tombstone is located atop the ride on the western side of Oakland. *Photograph by Gary D. Joiner.*

It was locally known as "the Pest House," for that is where consumption or tuberculosis patients were quarantined.

During a time of major crisis in Louisiana, at the peak of the Civil War, Egan was responsible for overseeing the establishment of a state laboratory at Mount Lebanon to produce medicines not only for the military but also for the civilian population. He supervised the creation of a distillery for "medicinal whiskey," a castor oil factory and a facility to produce "indigenous medicines."[31] The work at Mount Lebanon under Dr. Egan's supervision was ahead of its time. His research concentrated on development of new pharmaceutical compounds and better treatment methods for the sick and wounded. Here Egan learned that the native poppy of Louisiana was as effective in offering pain relief as imported opium.[32] He also cultivated hemp as a substitute for rope.

Egan married Ann Cormick in Ireland in 1817, and the couple had a son, William, who was listed on the 1850 census as living with them in Bienville Parish.[33] Egan's diligent work in advancing the cause of wartime medicine was equally matched in his concern for caring for the sick and dying among the civilian population. His practice of medicine continued in Shreveport after the war, and he had a great research interest in the yellow fever epidemic of 1873. Egan died at the age of eighty-three in 1879, and his marker in Oakland is a simple headstone noting his Irish heritage.

Claiborne Lee Foster

Son of Claiborne Jasper Foster and first cousin of John Gray Foster (both chronicled separately in this volume), Claiborne Lee Foster was born in 1865 in Shreveport as the Civil War was coming to a close and a new era of renewed westward expansion was underway. Following his education in Shreveport, Claiborne attended West Point Military Academy from June 15, 1884, to June 11, 1888. After he graduated, he was commissioned as a second lieutenant in the U.S. Army.[34] His first assignment was a second lieutenant in the 11th Infantry Regiment. His next assignment in Troop G of the 5th Cavalry

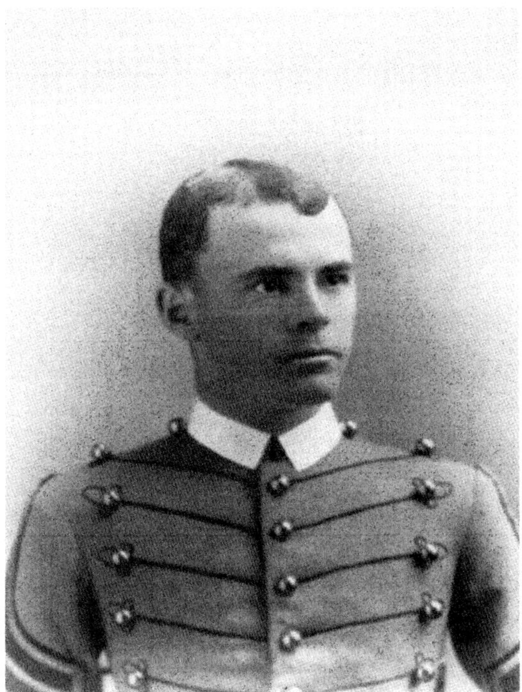

Claiborne Lee Foster is pictured here in his U.S. Military Academy at West Point senior portrait (1888). *LSU Shreveport, Noel Memorial Archives.*

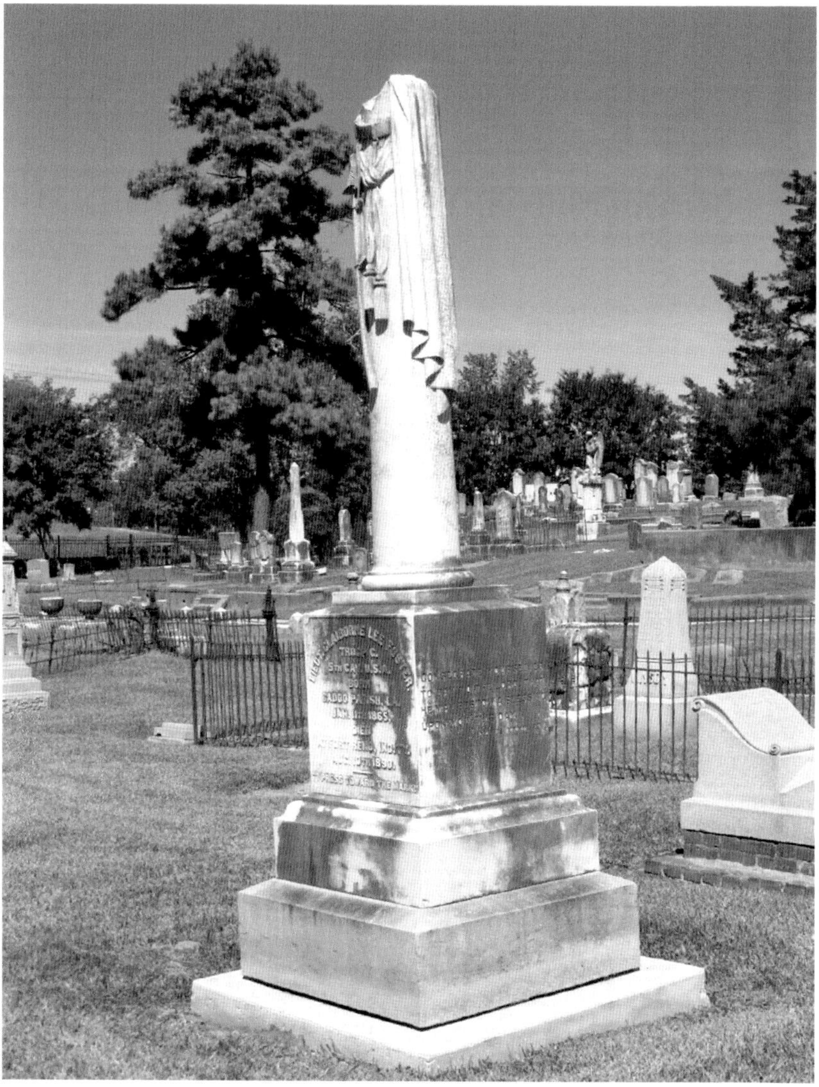

Claiborne Lee Foster's heroic column monument has an unfinished column top with a drape, his officer's sash and a sword. *Photograph by Gary D. Joiner.*

Regiment took him to the Indian Territory at Fort Reno, Oklahoma, where he met his death at the young age of twenty-five in 1890.[35] Like many other families of the age, the Fosters suffered the loss of more than one child to violence or illness at an early age. In addition to the murder of John Gray Foster at the age of twenty-three, the family had other losses of very young children: Erastus Foster at the age of four, Ernest Foster at the age of two, and Blanchard Foster at the age of one. All are buried together in a large family plot at Oakland.

Fort Reno, near the current town of El Reno, in the west central Indian Territory, was a notable assignment for Claiborne Foster upon his graduation from West Point, but it came at a time of great transition in history. Fort Reno was established in 1874 as a means of keeping peace for the diversity of native tribes in the area, taking its name from General Jesse Reno, a Civil War hero for the Union. It was to extend control over the reservations of the Cheyenne and Arapaho, and forces from Fort Reno had frequently seen armed conflict throughout the 1870s and 1880s.[36] The soldiers of Fort Reno had not only maintained the peace among the natives but also worked to keep out other settlers who surged in the territory as part of the "Boomer" invasion. The fort played an important role in the transition to Oklahoma statehood, and with stability in the region, the reasons for the fort's establishment ceased to exist. In fact, Oklahoma became a U.S. territory in 1890, the same year Foster died.

It was during the opening of Oklahoma for settlement that Claiborne Foster seems to have stood out among his fellow officers at Fort Reno. He and a small group of men were able to hold back a large group of settlers pushing into reservation lands, an event that was reported in newspapers as far away as New York. This he seemingly accomplished with only words and no use of force.[37]

A memorial for him published soon after his death notes that "there were no negative qualities in his make-up. His mental and physical conditions were reflections the one of the other—both indicative of robust strength." Yet despite his youth and vigor, Claiborne came down with a high fever that was undiagnosed, and death claimed him at Fort Reno, where witnesses reported he uttered one final word: "happy."[38] His death while in military service at a young age is the reason for Foster's most unusual marker at Oakland Cemetery. It depicts an unfinished column, with an officer's sash and sheath draped over it, symbolizing a young hero.

Captain James Martin Foster

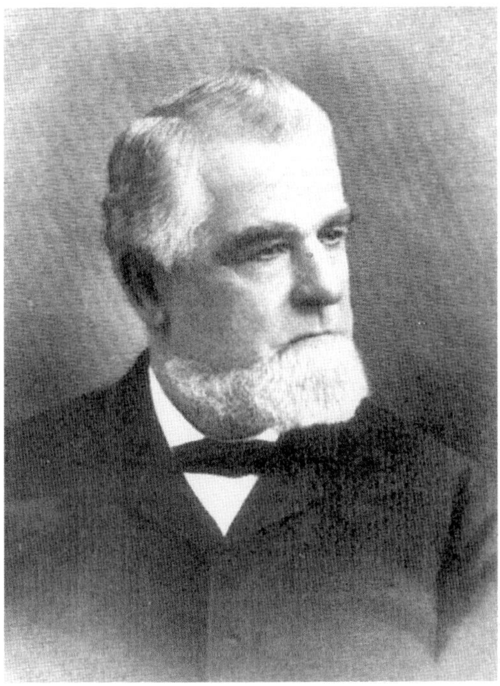

This image of James Martin Foster is from the height of his power and prestige. *Image from Lilla McLure and J. Ed Howe,* History of Shreveport and Shreveport Builders, *290.*

James Martin Foster arrived in Caddo Parish at the young age of ten when his farming parents relocated to the fertile Red River lands from Monroe County, Alabama, in 1841. He pursued academic study in civil engineering at the Western Military Institute in Kentucky before returning to the area in 1859 to continue in the cotton business that his father had begun. Foster could not have known that his decision to turn away from engineering pursuits in favor of returning home would figure so prominently in the history of the region. He returned to Caddo Parish on the eve of the Civil War, and the Foster family plantation placed him geographically near the major activity of the Red

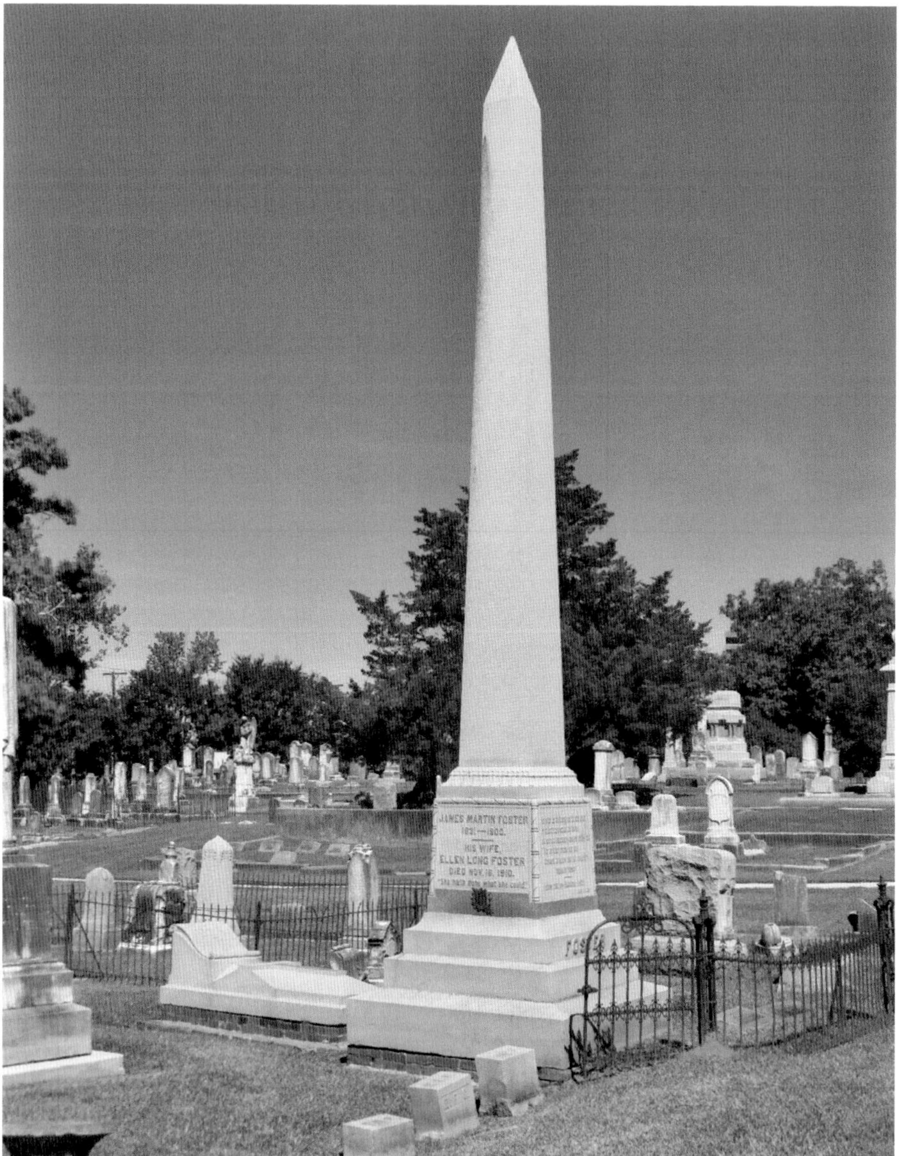

James Martin Foster's grand obelisk monument is the largest in Oakland. *Photograph by Gary D. Joiner.*

River Campaign of 1864, when Union general Nathaniel Banks advanced on Shreveport. Following the Battle of Mansfield, the Foster plantation served as a hospital for the wounded and dying.[39] In the aftermath of the war, Foster and his brother, Captain Claiborne Jasper Foster, were among the early few who were able to successfully make the challenging transition from an economy of slave labor to one modeled on free labor.[40] The Foster plantation was the largest in the region, with properties on both sides of the Red River. The largest single portion encompasses all of Barksdale Air Force Base today and extends west to the Red River and east to beyond Louisiana Downs. James Foster also owned New Egypt and Little Egypt plantations.[41]

A prominent figure within the state Democratic Party, Foster emerged as a natural leader during the precarious Reconstruction period in Louisiana and again during the scandalous Louisiana Lottery affair of 1892. He was a man who was known for his strong principles and sense of prevailing personal integrity, attributes that made him the longest-serving president of the Caddo Parish Police Jury with a record eight terms in that office. This tenure amounted to laudable community service, as he reportedly donated the salary he received to the Genevieve Orphanage in Shreveport.[42]

Foster married Ellen Long of Natchitoches in 1859, and the couple had eleven children. One of their sons, John Gray Foster, is profiled separately herein. His wife, Ellen (or Nellie, as she was sometimes called), was also a community leader, serving as the first president of the Hypatia Club and the Pelican Chapter of the Daughters of the American Revolution. The prominence of the family is obvious from the statewide obituaries that honored Captain Foster, including a special editorial in the *Shreveport Times* that noted, "Another grand old hero of Louisiana and the South passes away."[43] His death on December 11, 1900, followed injuries sustained in a fall from a horse some months before that had gradually eroded his health. The plot he shares with his wife in Oakland Cemetery is marked by an interesting and amusing monument that memorializes both husband and wife. Perhaps as a final tribute to her husband or out of humble deference to her husband's stature and prominence, the inscription under Ellen's name reads, "She hath done what she could."

John Gray Foster

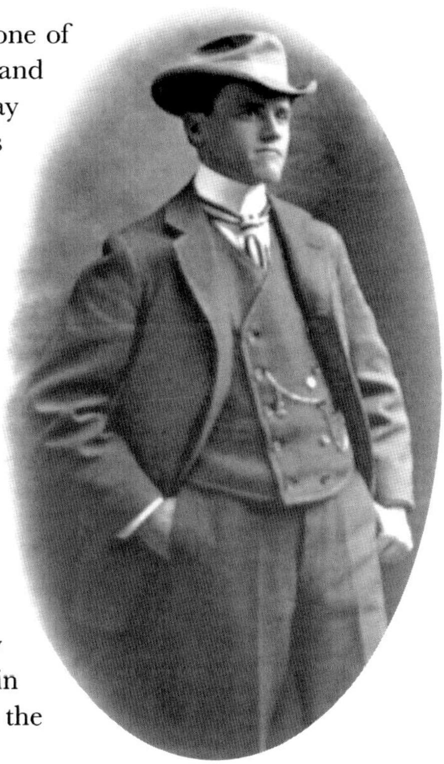

The son of James Martin Foster, one of the area's wealthiest planters and most influential citizens, John Gray Foster was only twenty-three years old and a recent alumnus of the University of Virginia when he was murdered on June 12, 1901, on the family estate in Bossier Parish. Because of the wealth and influence of the Foster family, the large plantation holdings were often the scene of disputes and conflicts with neighboring planters, as well as between laborers and their supervisors. The patriarch of the family, James Martin Foster, had died just a few months before, leaving sons John Gray Foster and his brother, James Martin Foster Jr., to take over and manage the

This image of John Gray Foster is from his memorial volume. *Collection of Mary T. McGuire.*

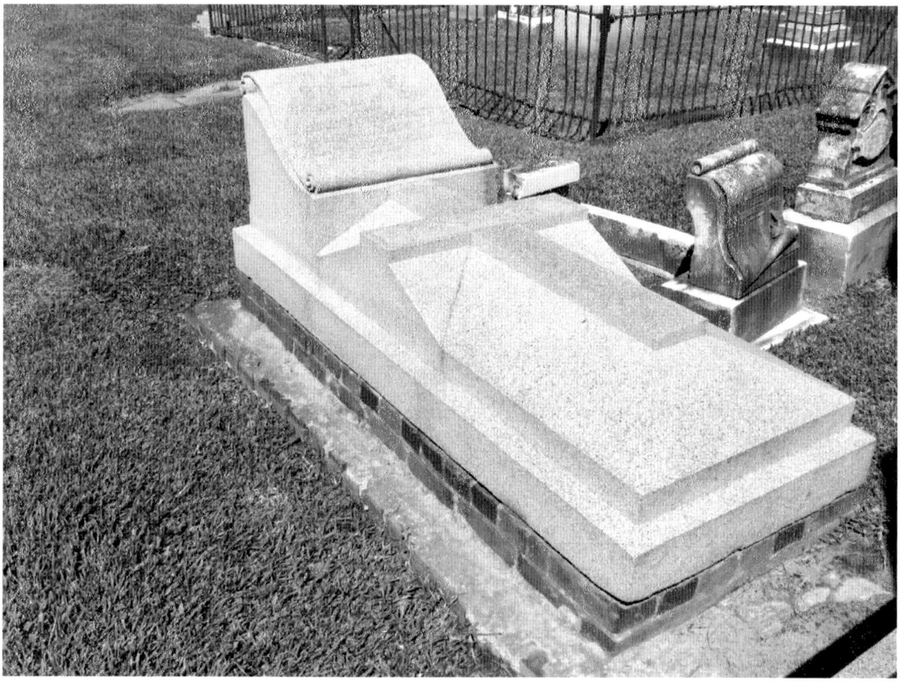

John Gray Foster's monument is in the style of a medieval knight with a scroll pillow and a large Latin cross placed above the body. *Photograph by Gary D. Joiner.*

family business. John Gray Foster came to the family cotton plantation in order to help resolve a dispute among workers, and it proved to be a fateful day for the young man who had only recently stepped into his father's shoes.

Accounts of the events of that day claim that Foster reprimanded a worker for drawing a pistol on his overseer. The worker then reportedly struck Foster in the head with a hoe or other farm tool with sufficient force that Foster retreated inside the plantation office to be treated. Later in the day, Foster and the overseer went to the laborer's cabin to fire him, and the worker opened fire with a shotgun, striking Foster in the chest and mortally wounding him.[44]

As expected, the area was outraged over the murder of Foster, and his death was reported in major city newspapers across the country. A manhunt involving hundreds of searchers ensued for the murderer, known as Prince Edwards, along a stretch of the Red River north of the Foster lands in Bossier Parish. Word then spread that Edwards, along with a cultic African American preacher known as Frank Smith (who called himself "the Prophet") and a fellow cult member named F.D. McLand, had taken refuge in the

Kinnebrew Store. The men belonged to a movement called the "Church of the Living God" and had apparently plotted the deaths of several prominent officials. Several hundred people surrounded the store and wanted to lynch the nearly twenty members of the church who sought refuge within its walls. They were eventually allowed to leave after Mr. Kinnebrew pleaded with the mob to not burn down his store.[45] A search of Smith's rooms found an objected called "the Ark of the Covenant," which was marked by crude, unknown symbols and contained evidence of further plots.[46] Prince Edwards was never found, but Bossier Parish indicted him on charges of murder in January 1902.[47] However, Smith and McLand were moved to the Bossier Parish jail. On the night of June 15, an angry mob of around two hundred men stormed the jail and forcibly took the two men about one mile north of Benton on Arkansas Road and lynched them.[48] The area was still driven by a rough vigilante justice mentality at the turn of the twentieth century.

It was a bizarre ending to a young life full of promise. Following a funeral at First Presbyterian Church, John Gray Foster was interred at Oakland Cemetery, with his name engraved on the large obelisk that marks the Foster family plot.

William Walton George

Shreve Town had humble beginnings in 1835, but the promise of prosperous commerce on the newly navigable Red River brought many to the area. On March 20, 1839, the Louisiana legislature officially incorporated the previous village of Shreve Town as Shreveport and gave full authorization for the city to begin operating under its own constituted government. The new city would have a mayor, five trustees, a treasurer, an assessor, a tax collector and various other administrative posts that might become necessary. The term of office for all elected officials was one year, and all male citizens aged twenty-one or older with a residency in the area of at least six months were eligible to vote. This legislative provision explains why some early Shreveport mayors and other officials have tenures in office that extended no more than one year.[49]

Among the first four trustees of the new city government was Dr. William Walton George, who served Shreveport in an interesting variety of roles. Besides his service as one of the first trustees, George was the first president of the Shreveport Medical Society, and he also served as Shreveport's second mayor in 1840. In 1842, George was elected to two more consecutive terms as mayor. He was also one of the first deacons for the First Baptist Church.[50] He is an example of the hardworking spirit that accompanied the frontier town's earliest permanent settlers, those willing to contribute in many diverse ways to the development and nurture of the fledgling river port.

Dr. George, born in 1807, was a native of Georgia, and he graduated with a doctor of medicine degree from Transylvania University in Lexington,

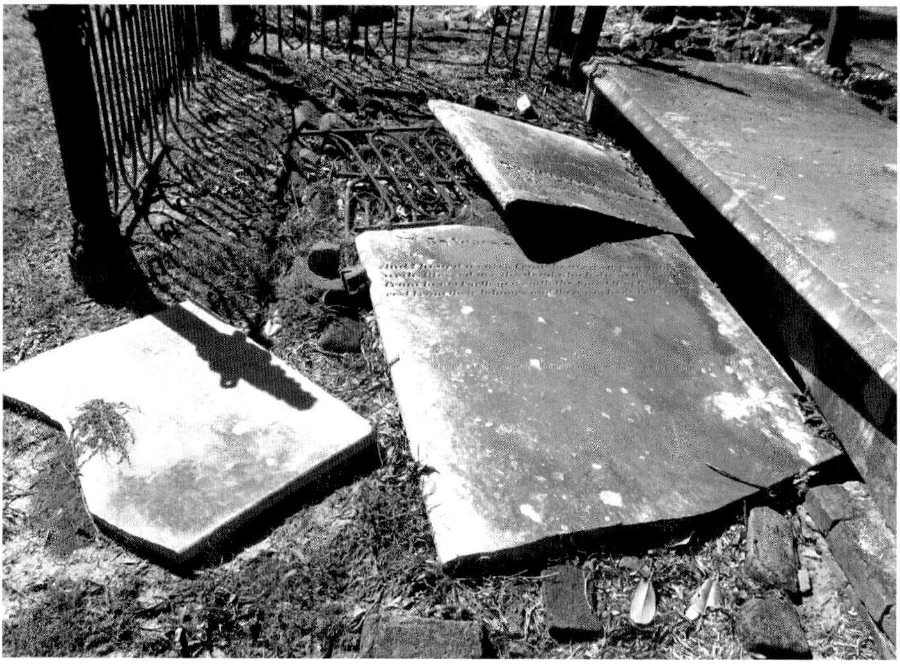

Broken basal tombstone of William W. George. *Photograph by Gary D. Joiner.*

Kentucky, in 1832. He married Mary Frances Battle in 1834. The couple had no children. There was an 1857 fire that destroyed his medical office near Texas and Market Streets,[51] and it appears that Dr. George primarily practiced frontier-style medicine by making house calls, since there were no hospitals known to exist in the city prior to the Civil War. In 1861, Dr. George was one of four candidates for the Louisiana House of Representatives,[52] but he lost the election.

He died in New York City in 1865 under unknown circumstances, but clearly, the couple was still making Shreveport home, as his body was returned to Shreveport for burial. Mary died in 1899 and rests beside her husband in Oakland Cemetery, both with flat markers covering their graves.

Nathan Goldkind

The grave of Nathan Goldkind in Oakland Cemetery might have the most compelling history associated with it. Nathan Goldkind (born Nussan ben Itzhak Goldkind in 1849) was a Polish immigrant who came to Shreveport by way of New York City with the intention of becoming a businessman. He first worked at Scopena Plantation in Bossier Parish, where he operated the plantation store before moving to Shreveport in 1879. Goldkind opened up a dry goods store, a two-story brick structure where he also lived, located on the corner of Common and Milam Streets.

Goldkind was an avid gambler who, at the time of his untimely death at the age of thirty-six, already bore several notable scars from the vice, including knife wounds and a missing left middle finger, which had been blown off in a shooting. Early on a Sunday morning in June 1885, Goldkind was playing cards in his store with a group of men, including another gambler named Gus Logan, who believed Goldkind to be cheating. Logan grabbed Goldkind's pistol and shot him through the eye. Goldkind died instantly.[53]

A Caddo District court found Gus Logan guilty of murder and sentenced him to death by hanging. However, Louisiana governor Samuel Douglas McEnery commuted Logan's capital sentence, giving him a life sentence of hard labor instead.[54] Yet in the nineteenth century, a "life sentence" often meant anything but, and Logan was freed from prison after serving only about four years. The Jewish community of Shreveport was outraged at the leniency that had been shown in Logan's case.

Shreveporter Louis Liebman paid for a unique tribute that memorialized his friend Nathan Goldkind but also vilified his murderer—a "white bronze" (zinc) marker that is boldly inscribed with the convicting words: "Nathan Goldkind, a native of Plotsk, Russian Poland. Killed in Shreveport, Louisiana by Gus Logan, June 14, 1885, Aged 36 Years." From that point forward, all passersby clearly saw the name of Gus Logan as Goldkind's murderer, as the marker was in clear view of Baker Street on the east side of the cemetery. Although Baker Street is no longer there, these damning words are etched in metal, and Goldkind's grave makes for an interesting stop for anyone walking through Oakland Cemetery today. The bottom of Goldkind's unique marker is further inscribed with the words, "In God He Trusted."

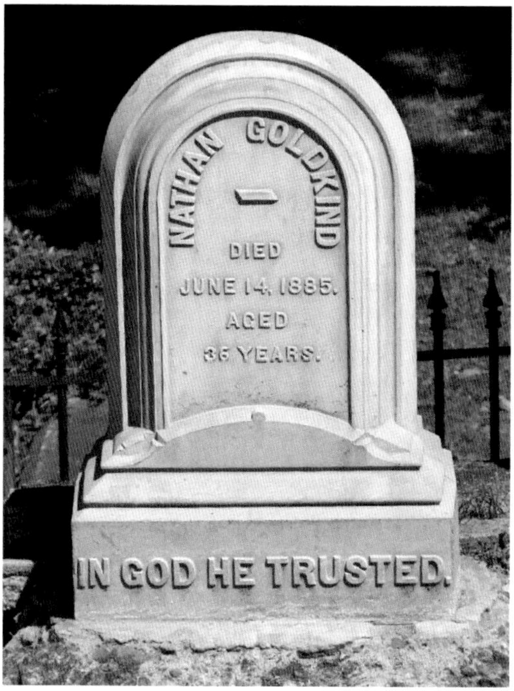

Top: White bronze (zinc) monument (west facing) of Nathan Goldkind. *Photograph by Gary D. Joiner.*

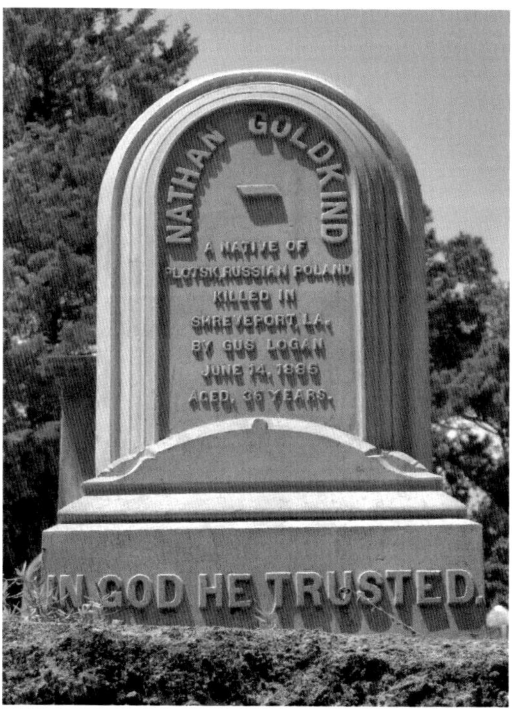

Left: White bronze (zinc) monument (east facing) of Nathan Goldkind. Note that the Baker street side tells all the passersby who murdered Goldkind and that justice was denied the young shopkeeper. *Photograph by Gary D. Joiner.*

John Lee Gooch

Within the story of Oakland Cemetery are occasionally found poignant reminders of lost chapters of city history. While it seems unlikely that prominent citizens would be among those pages of lost history, there are nevertheless a few notable examples. Mayor of Shreveport during the crucial years of 1864–65, just as the Civil War was coming to a close and north Louisiana was the target of a Union advance in the Red River Campaign, John Lee Gooch left behind only sketchy information about his life. Sadly, the final details of his life and death are wrapped in even greater obscurity, as the exact location of his burial within Oakland Cemetery is unknown. His grave is unmarked, and information about his death and funeral are also incomplete.

It is believed that Gooch was a native of Mississippi and was probably born in 1828. He married Matilda (Mattie) Sterrett in 1855, and the couple is listed on the 1860 U.S. census with two children living in Shreveport, but by the time of the 1870 census, the couple reported having an only son named Lee, age seven. Matilda Sterrett was a daughter of Alexander Boyd Sterrett, the first sheriff of Caddo Parish.

The historical record does reveal that John Lee Gooch was the defendant in a lawsuit brought by his siblings over aspects of their mother's estate in 1872 and that this case reached the Louisiana Supreme Court.[55] Because of that record, we know that Gooch had at least one brother named Thomas Gooch and that their mother was named Martha Gooch. Much of the remainder of Mayor Gooch's life remains a mystery, as do the circumstances surrounding his death in 1877. Even the Shreveport City Council records relating to affairs within the cemetery are sparse for the years 1875–78, with no entries in the record at all during 1877.[56] The site of his grave is unknown, but it is believed he is buried within Oakland Cemetery near his wife, Matilda. They may be resting near the remainder of the Sterrett family, whose grave locations are also unknown.

James Madison Hollingsworth

This Confederate hero of the Battle of Shiloh reached the rank of lieutenant colonel in the 19th Louisiana Regiment.[57] Hollingsworth came to Louisiana from his native Alabama in 1840 and later finished his formal schooling at the Western Military Institute in Kentucky. His social and educational background naturally drew him into military service on behalf of the Confederacy in 1861. Following the war's conclusion, Hollingsworth vigorously pursued the life of a planter in the region, with farmland located in Caddo, Bossier and DeSoto Parishes. His marriage to Elizabeth Key Quarles in 1859 produced three children.[58]

Hollingsworth is further noted for his radical politics, as he is credited with being one of the primary organizers of the White League in Shreveport. In 1874, the local chapter of this statewide paramilitary group began to operate. It was primarily an association forged among former Confederate soldiers committed to the political structure of the "Old South." The Louisiana White League began in St. Landry Parish and quickly spread to other parts of the state. The groups worked to restore the old southern Democratic Party to power and often used tactics of intimidation against Republican candidates, former slaves and any officeholder or representative of the Reconstruction government.[59] Unlike the Knights of the White Camellia or the Ku Klux Klan, the White League was not a secret society and grew rapidly by issuing emotional public appeals to former Confederates and Democrats to join.

There are dramatic examples in Louisiana history of the White League's violent clashes. In Coushatta in 1874, six Republican officeholders were killed after being promised safe passage to Texas if they would abandon their offices. Also, in the same year, New Orleans witnessed what became known as the Battle of Liberty Place, following a White League purchase of a shipment of arms that arrived in the city on the steamboat *Mississippi*. When the state militia tried to intercept the arms shipment, a battle ensued, but it proved to be one in which the White League prevailed.[60] The organization clearly sent a message that Republican Reconstruction policies would not hold in Louisiana without armed resistance. Hollingsworth was the first leader of the White League in Shreveport and was dedicated to the same principles. Estimates regarding the strength of the White League across north Louisiana stand at around ten thousand men, and the *Shreveport Times* published editorials prompting men to join.[61] The overall goal of the White League was to force Republican Reconstructionists to adopt the white supremacist politics of the Democratic Party or "be driven from the country and killed."[62] The White League ceased to operate within a few years

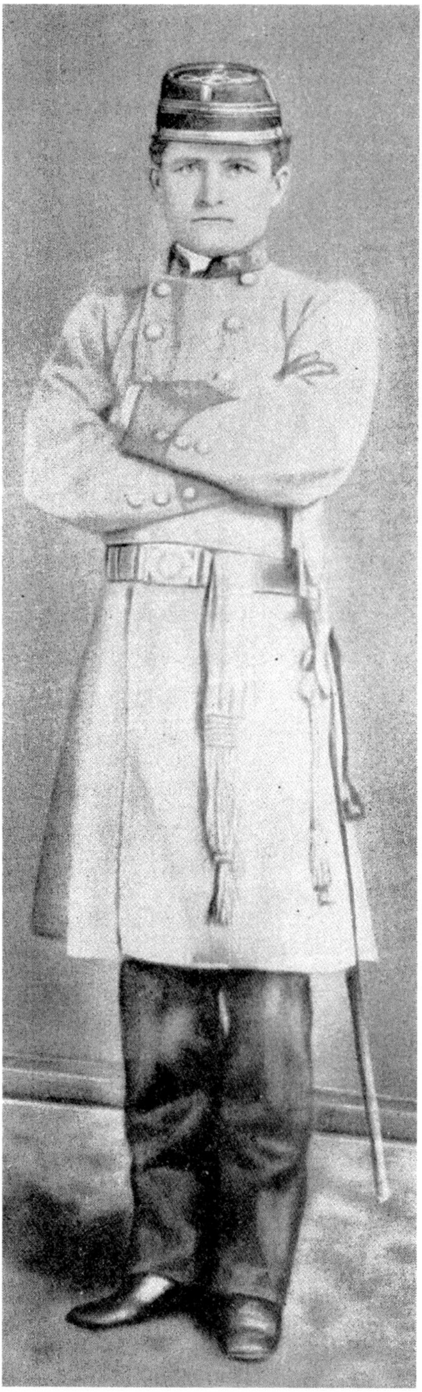

James Hollingsworth poses in his confederate uniform. *Image from Lilla McLure and J. Ed Howe,* History of Shreveport and Shreveport Builders, *258.*

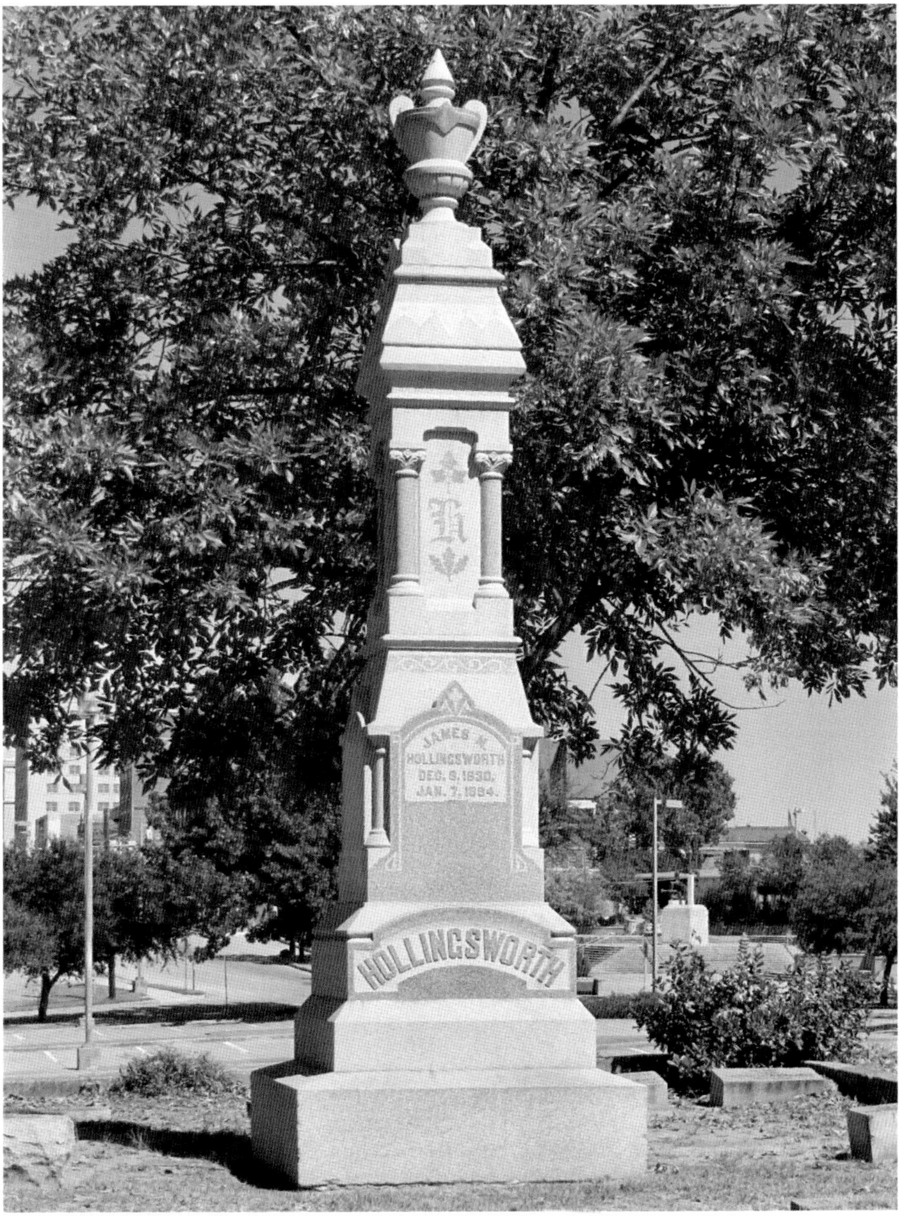

James Hollingsworth's monumental granite obelisk has Greco-Roman and Byzantine influences. *Photograph by Gary D. Joiner.*

of its formation, but the return of Louisiana to its prewar Democratic status is at least partially due to the intimidation and violent tactics of the organization. It was largely responsible for turning an enforced pro-Republican electorate into the "Solid [Democratic] South" that lasted until the 1970s."

Hollingsworth died in 1894 and is buried in Oakland Cemetery, his grave marked by a distinguished monument with Corinthian columns and a large urn at the top. He is buried next to daughter Pearl, who died in infancy in 1872.

Thomas P. Hotchkiss

Near the eastern wall of Oakland Cemetery and just south of Hebrew Rest No. 1 lies a ground tablet marker that reads, "Thomas P Hotchkiss, Surg F&S 1 LA Cavalry, Confederate States Army, Sep 2 1814 Oct 8 1873." This somewhat cryptic epitaph understates a remarkable life. Thomas P. Hotchkiss was a native of Vermont, but he moved to Shreveport before its incorporation. He was both a trained physician and an engineer. His fellow immigrants elected him as one of the first trustees, or council members, of Shreveport in 1839. The 1850 census lists him as a practicing physician, age thirty, living with his wife and three children.[63] During the 1850s, Hotchkiss also was among the founders of the local Masonic lodge and was central to the founding of a navigation company and a railroad.

Hotchkiss used both his medical and engineering training during the Civil War. He formed and led a unit of Home Guards in Caddo Parish. The Confederate authorities appreciated his medical skills and showed it by appointing him to the rank of captain and medical officer, field and staff, of the 1st Louisiana Cavalry Regiment. His service records list him as being on duty in Bowling Green, Kentucky, under General Albert Sidney Johnston prior to the Battle of Shiloh and then in Richmond, Virginia, in March 1863. Incongruously, in the interim, he resigned from service in June 1862.[64] He then returned to northwest Louisiana, reentered Confederate service as an engineer working on the staff of General William R. Boggs. Hotchkiss's title was swampland commissioner, but his real duties involved the construction of secret dams at Tones Bayou, at the time about forty-five river miles below

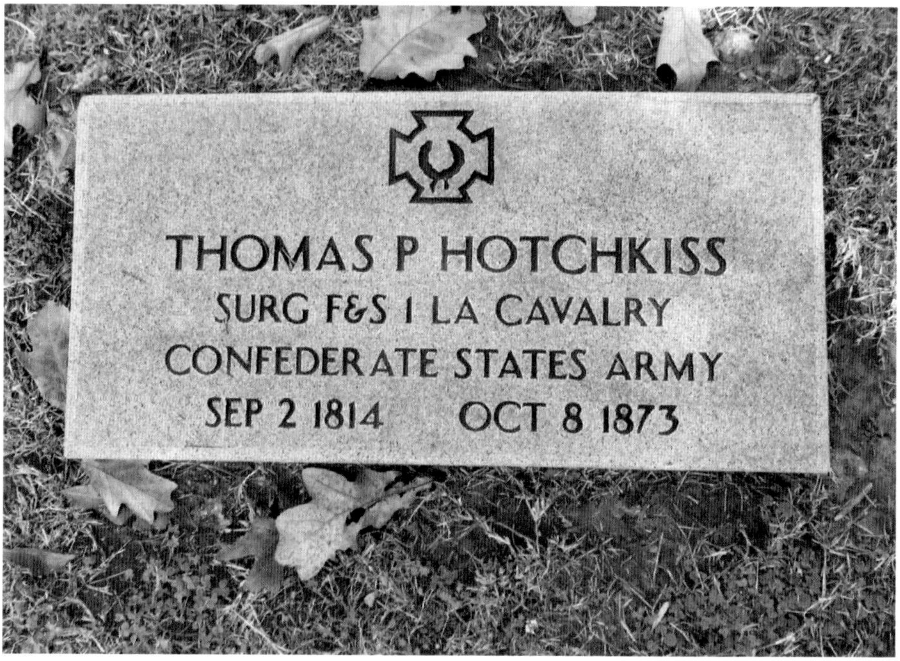

Thomas P. Hotchkiss's military-style ground tablet marker has a cross and wreath that identify him as a Confederate veteran. The "SURG F&S 1 LA CAVALRY" identifies him as a surgeon, field and staff officer of the First Louisiana Cavalry Regiment. *Photograph by Gary D. Joiner.*

Shreveport, today near the Port of Shreveport Bossier. A dam bearing his name became crucial in the Union efforts to divert the flow from the Red River into Bayou Pierre with the intention of trapping the Union navy as it ascended the river in 1864 to capture Shreveport.[65] The plan succeeded to a remarkable degree. As the Union fleet moved up the river to Alexandria and above, the water dropped precipitously. Fully three-quarters of the Red River's current was diverted into the side channel, almost stranding the bulk of the Union's inland navy.

Following the Civil War, Dr. Hotchkiss returned to the life of a physician. He was one of the most respected medical practitioners in the region. During the great yellow fever epidemic in the region in 1873, Hotchkiss was at the center of helping the stricken and dying. Shreveport lost fully one-fourth of its population in three weeks during the late summer and fall. Dr. Hotchkiss worked until he contracted the fever and died on October 8. He was mourned by the City of Shreveport and residents of the region.

John N. Howell

One of the most distinctive and impressive markers within Oakland Cemetery memorializes the life of one of Shreveport's earliest mayors. John N. Howell was mayor from 1845 to 1846, during the time when Oakland Cemetery was being established as the city burial grounds. Howell was therefore one of Shreveport's earliest permanent residents, coming from North Carolina in 1840. He is listed as one of the incorporators of the Red River Navigation Company.[66] The Howell home, built in 1849, was one of the city's earliest residential structures at the corncr of Spring and Lake

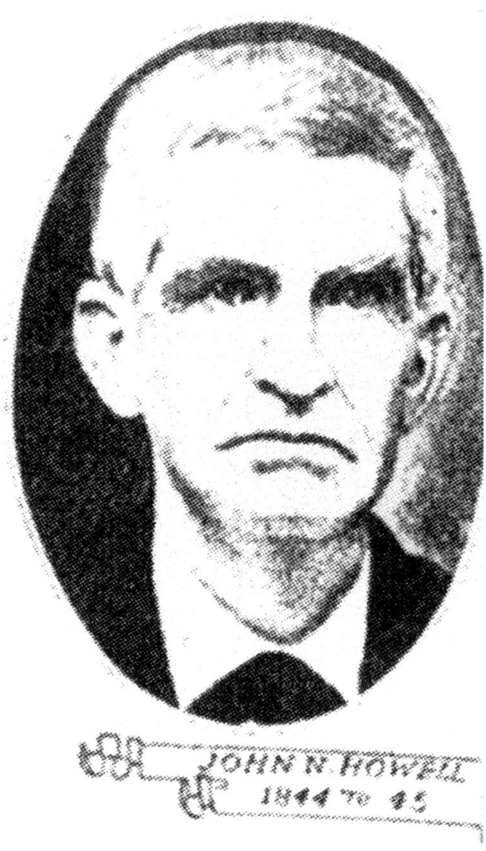

This image of John N. Howell is from a montage of early Shreveort mayors. *LSU Shreveport, Noel Memorial Archives.*

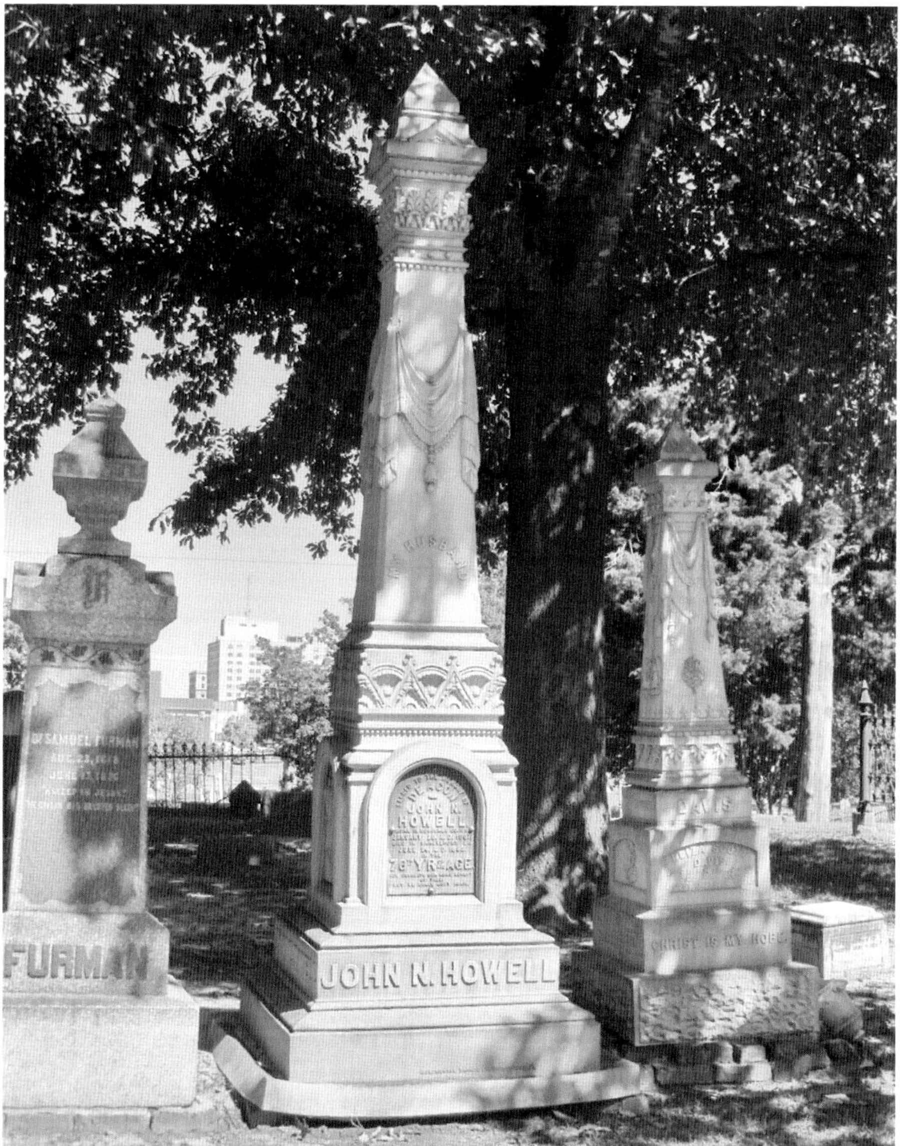

John N. Howell's white bronze (zinc) monumental column is the tallest such monument in Oakland. Seemingly every square foot of surface is covered by iconography. *Photograph by Gary D. Joiner.*

Streets, but of course, it is no longer standing. However, its construction in 1849 illustrates how lively the current downtown area was as a residential center in the early years of city history.

The Howell family was active in the emerging social scene of Shreveport. They also were fully engaged with early philanthropic efforts of the young city and were among the charter members of First Baptist Church when it organized in 1845. In fact, Howell was one of the first two deacons of the church.[67] Records also indicate that Howell provided foster care to numerous homeless children in Shreveport, with one count noting that Howell and his wife took in twenty-three children at varying points in time.[68]

When it came time to structure some system of higher education for the city in the immediate post–Civil War era, Howell was among the board of trustees for an entity known as Shreveport University, which was located on Texas Avenue near the intersection of Greenwood Road. Following the yellow fever epidemic of 1873, the school of higher learning began to dissolve as faculty and students fell ill, died or fled the area. The institution was forced to close in 1876, and when the buildings went up for auction at a sheriff's sale in 1877, John Howell purchased it for $1,500. He tore down the existing structures and repurposed the brick for the construction of a new First Baptist Church.[69]

Howell died in 1882 at the age of seventy-six and is buried in Oakland near his wife, Mary Jane Howell Furman, and his mother-in-law, Eliza Scott Davis. The interesting iconography of his marker includes a large anchor with the words, "My hope in Christ is strong" and "The steps of a good man are ordered by the Lord and he delighteth in His way."

Benjamin Jacobs

A native of Freinwalde, Prussia,[70] Benjamin came to America in 1842 to join his brother, Edward Jacobs, who had already set up residence and a business in Shreveport. Within just a few years, the brothers Jacobs had established a successful mercantile on Texas Street, appropriately titled E&B Jacobs and Company. The brothers enjoyed a diverse business, trading in everything from cotton to tobacco, but also developed a fortuitous interest in banking. In 1877, the E&B Jacobs Bank opened for business, and this institution later became the First National Bank of Shreveport.

The impact of the Jacobs family on Shreveport history is obvious in the tracing of the family tree. The brothers Benjamin and Edward married sisters, Amazona and Palestine Cole of Blanchard, respectively. Their success in business, level of community engagement and response to civic duty is all well documented in the story of this city, and was passed to future generations of the Jacobs family. Benjamin served as treasurer of the Cotton Exchange and was also a director of the Shreveport Coast Navigation Company, which transported goods from Shreveport to New Orleans in the 1870s.[71]

Records indicate that Benjamin Jacobs's wealth was of sufficient standing for him to be the recipient of a presidential pardon for activities during the Civil War. President Andrew Johnson signed the pardon on September 26, 1866, citing that Benjamin Jacobs, "by taking part in the late rebellion against the Government of the United States, has made himself liable to heavy pains and penalties; and whereas, the circumstances of his case render him a proper object of Executive clemency."[72] There were, of course, economic

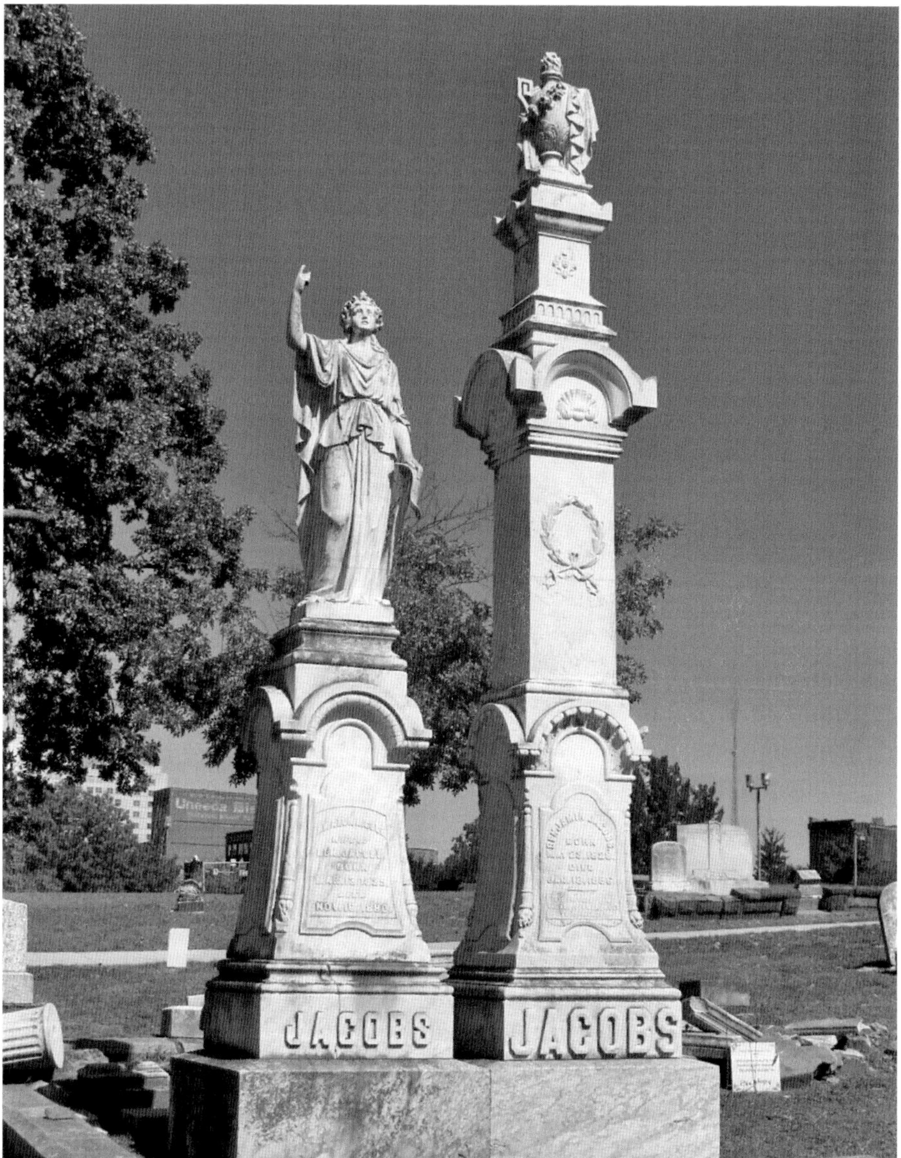

These exquisite double marble monuments for Amazona Cole Jacobs and Benjamin Jacobs are by far the most detailed and wonderfully carved monuments in Oakland. *Photograph by Gary D. Joiner.*

motivators for men like Jacobs to actively seek a presidential pardon after the war, since any property that had been taken by the federal government during hostilities could not otherwise be reclaimed. By the end of 1865, pardons were coming out of President Johnson's office at the rate of over one hundred per day; by the time that Jacobs's was issued in 1866, over seven thousand women had property restored due to executive clemency.[73]

Jacobs and his wife, Amazona, had several children, but only two lived to adulthood. Amazona predeceased Benjamin, dying in 1880, and the couple is buried side by side in a remarkable family plot in Oakland Cemetery. Their monuments are among the most beautiful and distinguished within Oakland and remain in excellent condition today. His marker, characteristically larger than his wife's, is inscribed with his birth date of May 23, 1828, and his date of death as January 18, 1886. His monument also bears an appropriate epitaph: "His virtues form the noblest monument to his memory." Both monuments are Greco-Roman motifs filled with religious and heroic themes. Amazona's features a goddess facing west with one arm raised and an index finger pointing toward Texas. On her elegantly quaffed hair is a tiara with a single Texas star.

Edward Jacobs

Born Ephraim Jacobi in Freienwalde, Prussia, in 1822, this immigrant to Louisiana became one of the pillars of early banking and commerce in Shreveport by the 1850s. As a young man, he crossed the Atlantic in 1842 and found his way to New Orleans, where he shed his Old World identity for the name of Edward Jacobs. Realizing the commercial opportunity that existed in the fledgling Red River port, Jacobs came to Shreveport a couple of years later.

His brother, Benjamin, also came from Germany to join him in business, and together they established E&B Jacobs and Company, a successful mercantile on Texas Street. There was no aspect of commerce that the Jacobs did not have an interest in, including cotton, furs, tobacco, real estate and banking. Each area of interest supported the other; it was an interest in cotton that led Jacobs to purchase large amounts of warehouse space in downtown Shreveport. By the time of the Civil War, Jacobs was significant in assisting with the passage through the city of goods headed to other Confederate supply hubs.[74]

Jacobs's venture into the banking business resulted in the creation of several area financial institutions. This legacy is still visible today in an early banking location, established at 525 Spring Street and still standing today as the Spring Street Museum. The earliest records available for this property indicate that a transfer took place in 1865, but it is unclear whether the building stood on the site at that time. However, the transfer of the property

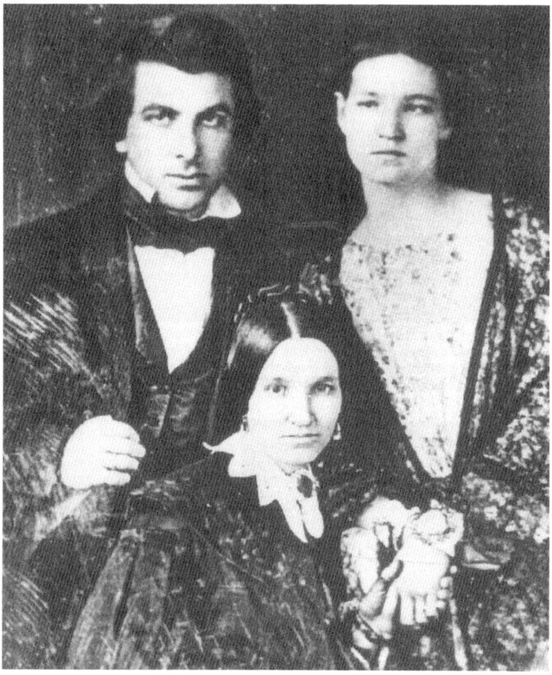

Photograph portrait of Edward Jacobs; Palestine Cole Jacobs (seated); and her sister, Amazona Cole Jacobs (wife of Benjamin Jacobs). *LSU Shreveport, Noel Memorial Archives.*

to Dew Talley in 1866 signaled its first use as a bank, and it became the property of Edward Jacobs in 1877.[75] This was the forerunner of what became a most successful banking business, the First National Bank, once said to have "the patronage of the largest firms, the most prominent and wealthy citizens, and also the surrounding country."[76] The bank occupied three separate locations in Shreveport, ever expanding in size and influence, to occupy the corner of Market and Milam Streets. It is the oldest bank incorporated in Louisiana.[77]

Jacobs's marriage to Palestine Cole of Alabama produced twelve children, six of whom lived to adulthood. His son Walter B. Jacobs followed his father into the banking business and served as second president of First National Bank. There are records of the Jacobs family's contributions to the community during the yellow fever outbreak of 1873, including the donation of cash sums to help with food and supplies at the peak of the epidemic.[78] The Jacobses made their family home in a Victorian mansion that stood at the corner of Travis and McNeill Streets, and that structure is reputed to have been the largest mansion in Shreveport at the time it was built in 1886. There are, unfortunately, few surviving examples of this era in Shreveport architecture, and the Jacobs home is no exception. In 1922, the home was torn down to allow construction of the YMCA on its site.

Although Jewish and a founding member of B'nai Zion Temple, Jacobs is buried within the nonsectarian section of Oakland Cemetery. Upon

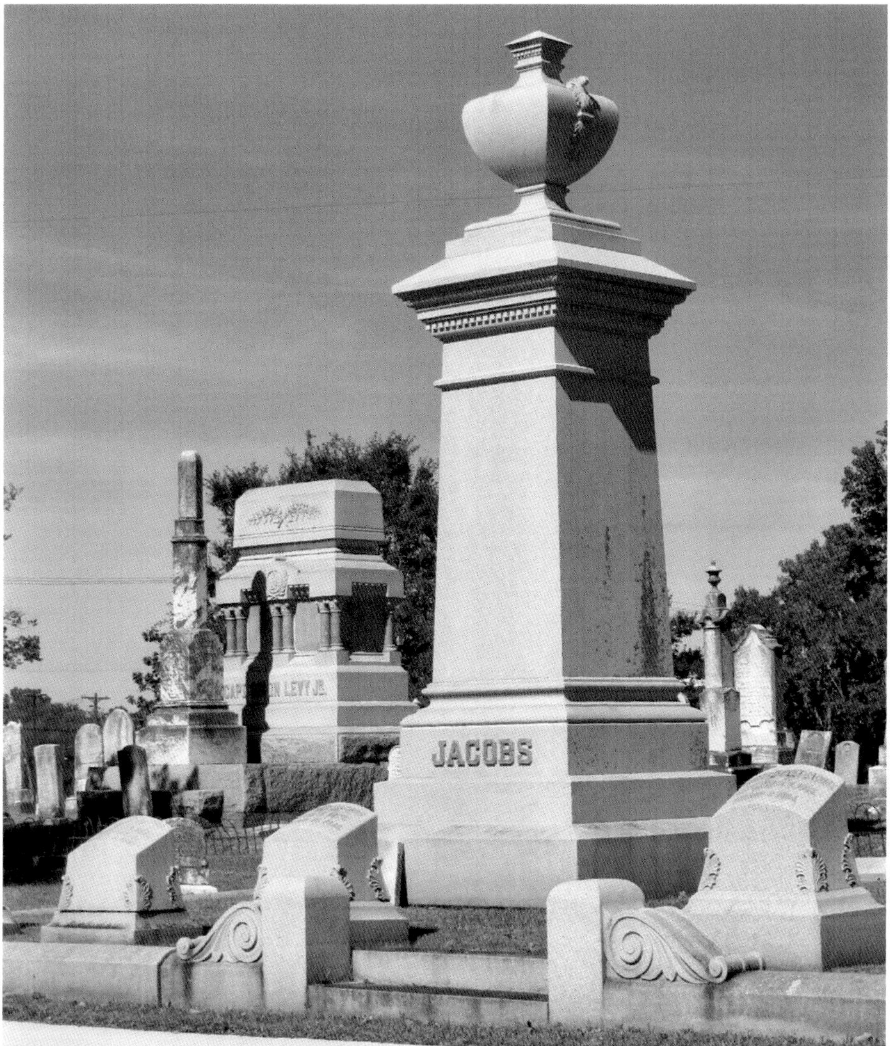

In the grand Edward Jacobs family plot at Oakland, the large cenotaph marks the center of the plot with each member having a matching scrolled marker. The large Simon Levy Jr. monument is to the left rear. *Photograph by Gary D. Joiner.*

his death in 1896, he was buried in a prominent family plot, marked by a monument that recognizes the family's stature and legacy in Shreveport history. The plot was previously a portion of a city street within the cemetery. Today, its long, narrow shape is due to that former use.

Roland Jones

One of the most damaged and endangered grave plots in Oakland Cemetery belongs to early Shreveporter Roland Jones and his wife, Annie Neville Stokes Jones. Roland Jones, born in North Carolina in 1813, was one of the original settlers at the time of Shreveport's incorporation and was a graduate of Cambridge Law School. His wife, Annie, was the daughter of North Carolina governor Montfort Stokes. The couple moved to Shreveport, where Jones established himself in a law career. He served in the Louisiana legislature in 1844 and was commissioned judge in Caddo Parish in 1851 and again in 1852.[79]

Jones was elected to serve as U.S. Representative for Louisiana's Fourth Congressional District from 1853 to 1855, making him an eyewitness to the brewing sectional controversies that would erupt into civil war in less than a decade. He served in national office at the time of the border wars between Kansas and Missouri that became known as "Bleeding Kansas" and began in 1854. The conflict had its origins in the issue of the expansion of slavery into new territories, something to be decided by "popular sovereignty" according to the Kansas-Nebraska Act of 1854, which created the new territories in the Midwest. The act effectively repealed the Missouri Compromise of 1820, which had sought to prohibit the expansion of slavery into new territories north and west of a line drawn from the Louisiana Purchase. As a U.S. congressman, Roland Jones was embroiled in this heated controversy, but he voted with other Southern Democrats in favor of allowing the issue of slavery to be decided by voters in the new territories.[80] The Kansas-Nebraska

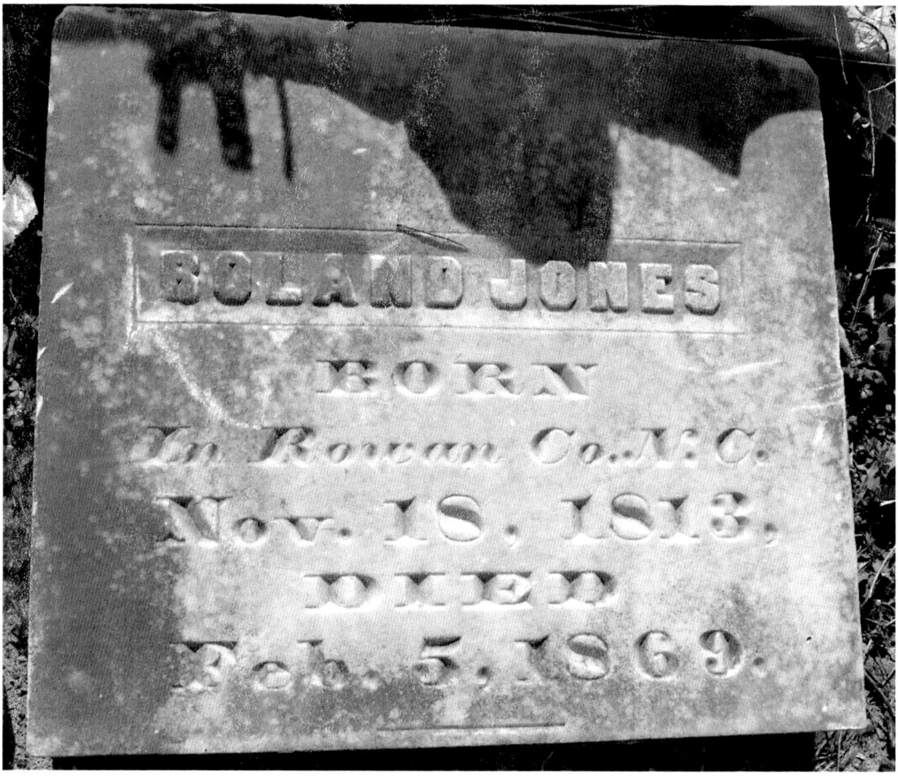

Roland Jones's broken monument. *Photograph by Pat Berel in Findagrave.com Monument No. 6954369.*

Act precipitated border clashes between settlers, resulting in the deaths of around one hundred people. It is hard to know, but perhaps this taste of political life soured Jones on future public service.

Roland Jones died in 1869; his wife, Annie, lived until 1895. They are buried next to each other in Oakland Cemetery, but their plot was heavily damaged by winds of a 2009 tornado that struck Shreveport. The poor condition of their monuments highlights the cemetery's need for an ongoing preservation and restoration effort. The Joneses' son, Montfort Stokes Jones, married Florence Burkett Jones. Florence became regionally famous as one of the "Angels of the Great Yellow Fever Epidemic." She was awarded by the Howard Association one of seven gold medals for her service to humanity.[81]

Isaac Kahn

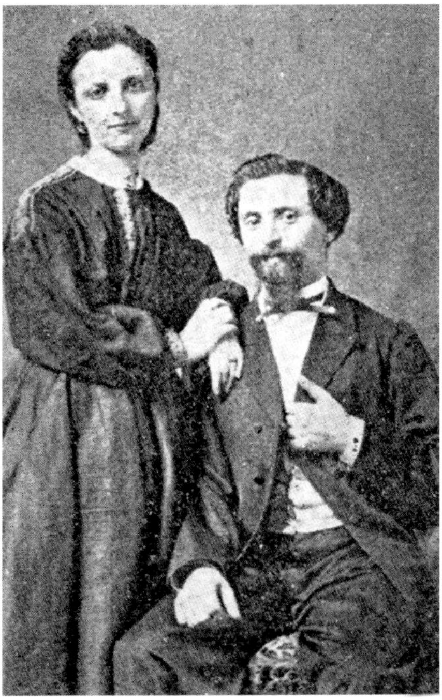

Image of Isaac Kahn and his wife, Fannie Kahn. *Image from Lilla McLure and J. Ed Howe,* History of Shreveport and Shreveport Builders, *227.*

One of the most prominent victims of the 1873 yellow fever epidemic in Shreveport, Isaac Kahn migrated to the United States from his native Alsace, France, as a young man, initially settling in Atlanta, Georgia, with his brothers Raphael and Julius. Like most young men, he answered the call to Confederate service when war broke out in 1861, and Kahn served with distinction. He was a member of the "Sumter Rifles" of the 24th Louisiana Infantry Regiment, entering service as a private and being discharged in 1865 after having reached the rank of sergeant. He had the further distinction of having survived being taken prisoner of war.[82]

In his brief life following the conclusion of the war, Kahn distinguished himself as a successful

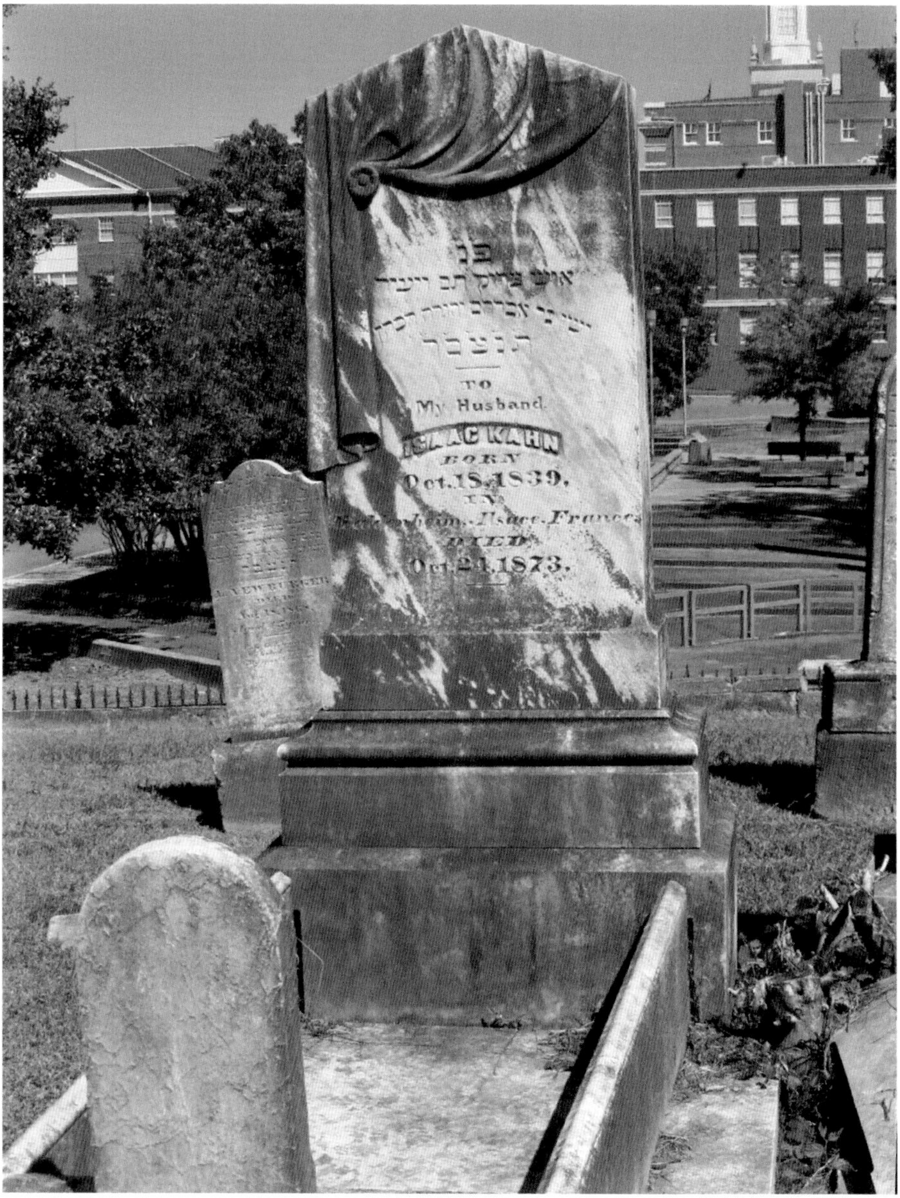

Isaac Kahn's large bedstead tomb is so called because fresh earth and annual flowers were planted between the bed rails and atop a marble slab. The construction resembles a large nineteenth-century bed with the monument forming the headboard. *Photograph by Gary D. Joiner.*

general merchandiser in Shreveport with an enterprise known as Kahn and Brothers. He and his wife, Fannie, had two sons who would grow up to also contribute to the ongoing civic life of Shreveport: son Leon was a city councilman, and son Arthur became president of Shreveport National Bank.[83] In 1873, when Shreveport was besieged by a particularly virulent yellow fever epidemic, tragedy struck the Kahn family multiple times. Isaac's brother Julius died of the disease on September 11. Just a week later, Isaac's son Bernard Benjamin ("Bennie"), age six, was also among the victims. Isaac Kahn fell ill just a few weeks following his son's death and succumbed to yellow fever on October 24. All three are buried in the Hebrew Rest section of Oakland Cemetery, but Isaac's marker alone bears the most obvious indicator of the family's grief. It is distinguished by a large drape, signifying mourning, and covers the entire top of the monument, also perhaps hinting at the thin veil between this life and the next. It is a poignant reminder that yellow fever exacted a particularly harsh price from this Shreveport family.

William Kinney

Strolling through Oakland Cemetery, the visitor will see many complex marble tombs and markers signed with variations of the word *Kinney* in block letters. William Kinney was the most prolific of three master stone carvers who worked in Shreveport. At times with partners but for most of his career alone, Kinney was a true master in his trade. Born in Limerick, Ireland, in 1836, he moved to the United States at the age of seventeen and then to Shreveport in 1856.[84]

When the Civil War began, Kinney volunteered quickly. His service began in May 1861 as a member of Company F, 3rd Louisiana Infantry. He quickly passed through the ranks, becoming an orderly sergeant. The following year, Kinney was voted captain of his company. The 3rd saw action in the first battle in the West, Oak Hill—or Wilson's Creek—Missouri, in August 1861, and then at Pea Ridge, or Elkhorn Tavern, in northwestern Arkansas. Following this, the 3rd moved to Mississippi,

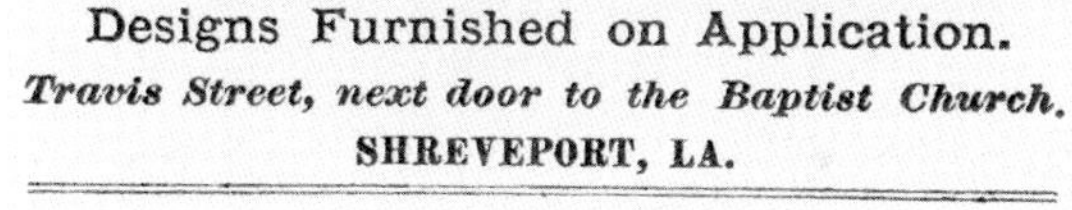

William Kinney was a master stone carver with a business in Shreveport, as shown by this advertisement. Kinney created more ornate tombstones and monuments in Oakland than any other individual. His work is also found in East Texas and western Louisiana. *Shreveport City Directory, 1875.*

where it was engaged at the Battle of Iuka. It played an important part in the siege of Vicksburg.[85] Following Kinney's parole, he returned to Louisiana at Alexandria. Kinney then was ordered to Shreveport, where he and the 3rd served in guarding the Confederate capital of Louisiana. After the war, he became one of the original members and the recording secretary of the General Leroy Stafford Camp of the United Confederate Veterans.

Kinney had apprenticed as a stonemason. Following the war, he built a business that catered to carving exquisite "foreign and domestic marble, monuments, head stones, tablets…terra cotta vases for cemetery and garden adornment." His shop was located on Travis Street next to the Baptist church, placing it in the block where Municipal Plaza is located today.[86]

William Kinney was a Roman Catholic and the recording secretary of the local Knights of Columbus. He achieved regional fame as the premier sculptor of funerary statuary in not only English but also Hebrew. Hebrew Rest No. 1, located in the northernmost portion of Oakland Cemetery, contains many of his finest works. Visitors to other cemeteries in the region will also discover Kinney's monuments. Examples are found in Greenwood, Hebrew Rest No. 2, Summer Grove and St. Joseph Cemeteries in Shreveport, as well as regional cemeteries in Bossier and DeSoto Parishes and Scottsville, Marshall and Karnack Cemeteries in east Texas.[87] Kinney never forgot his Confederate friends. His carved angels and figures of women are the most memorable of his efforts.

Strangely, his own marker is an inexpensive commercial marble, sold at the time by Sears, Roebuck & Company. Its information is faint, but one can still read his name and see a faded Confederate battle flag. The same is true for his wife. His son's statue, lying next to the carver's, was done by him and is a representation of a child. Kinney died in 1907, just as Oakland was filling up and the new Greenwood Cemetery was beginning to hit its stride as the primary city cemetery.

Thomas Thompson Land

A prominent figure in the legal field of both the city and the state of Louisiana, Thomas Thompson Land was born in Tennessee in 1815 and studied law at the University of Virginia. Prior to coming to Shreveport in 1846, Land served in the Mississippi legislature for four years before moving west to Texas (while it was still an independent republic). He settled in Shreveport in 1846 and established a law practice. In 1854, he became district judge for the combined jurisdictions of Caddo, Bossier and Desoto Parishes; by 1858, he had been elected a justice of the Louisiana Supreme Court, and the Land family moved to New Orleans. After Union forces occupied New Orleans in 1862, the Lands took refuge in Shreveport, and Thomas technically remained on the court until 1865, when he returned to Shreveport permanently and resumed a private practice of law.[88] He served the citizens of the city in that role until the politics of the Reconstruction era were over in the South and it was time to reconstitute state government.

When the Louisiana Constitutional Convention met in 1879, Land was a delegate representing Caddo Parish. This was the convention that met to return Louisiana to the status of "home rule" with a new state constitution following Reconstruction. Technically speaking, this constitution was supposed to bring about major changes for Louisiana following the guidelines of Reconstruction, including the creation of a free public education system and an article that clearly stated there would be no restrictions on suffrage "based on race, color, or previous condition of servitude."[89] However, elsewhere in the articles, there were signals of an intent to maintain the pre–Civil War status quo, including

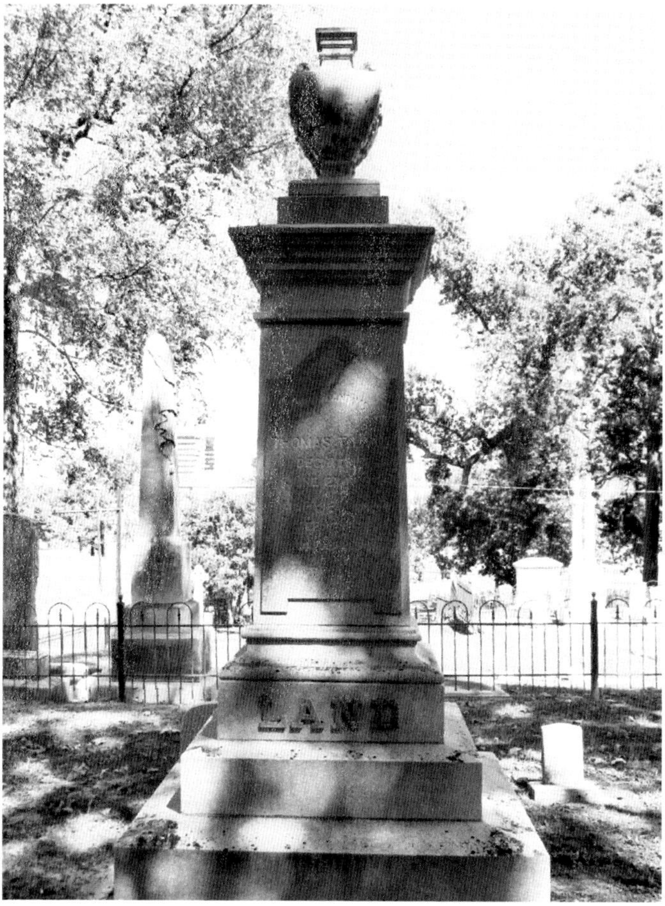

Thomas Land's grand column monument dominates the northwestern corner of the cemetery. *Photograph by Gary D. Joiner.*

the institution of a poll tax to fund free public education, which, of course, became notorious for its use in disenfranchising former slaves. This constitution also continued and expanded the corrupt Louisiana Lottery system.[90] Amid this complex time in state history, it is a testimony to Land's reputation that he was appointed to serve as the chairman of the prestigious judiciary committee of the convention, which oversaw the establishment and ordering of the Louisiana justice system under the new constitution.[91]

Land married Mary Eliza Dillingham of Mississippi in 1839, and the couple had fourteen children. The Land family plot at Oakland Cemetery is the final resting place for Justice Thomas Thompson Land, who died in 1893, as well as Mary, who died in 1901. Also buried within are seven of the Land children. The plot is one of the most picturesque spots in Oakland, surrounded by beautiful black iron fencing.

John Morgan Landrum

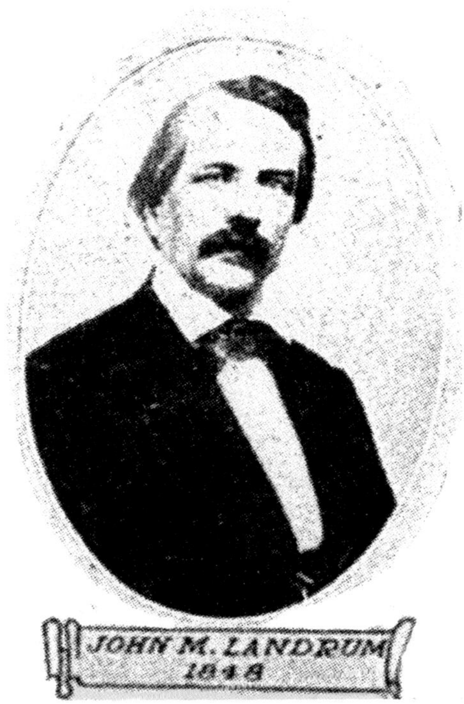

This image of John M. Landrum is from a montage of early Shreveport mayors. *LSU Shreveport, Noel Memorial Archives.*

John Landrum was mayor of Shreveport in 1848 and was actually one of the first mayors of Shreveport to oversee the city's ownership of the newly acquired Oakland Cemetery. Landrum's immediate predecessor, Robert Nathaniel Wood, was mayor at the time the property for Oakland was set aside as the city burial grounds, and the efforts to retain the land began with Wood's predecessor, Lawrence Pike Crain. Landrum also played an important role in the creation of the Louisiana Lake and Bayou Navigation Company in 1854, serving as the first secretary of the company. The purpose of this enterprise was "to construct a navigable passage for steamers and other boats around the Red River Raft and keep it free from

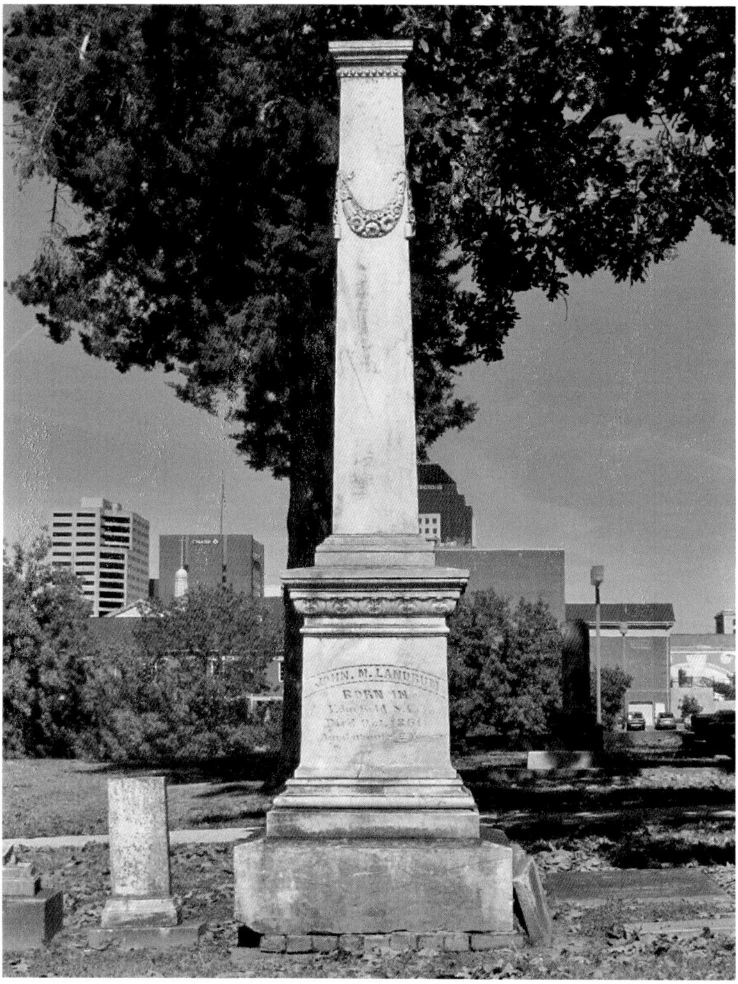

John M. Landrum's monumental column. *Photograph by Gary D. Joiner.*

obstructions."[92] The U.S. government was inconsistent in its commitment to maintain river navigability following its initial clearance by Captain Henry Miller Shreve, so private companies emerged with the stated objectives of helping to improve navigation and encourage more trade through the region. Therefore, Landrum's role in the early history of Shreveport was pivotal since the survival of the city was dependent on the success of making and keeping the waterway open to commerce.

Landrum was a native of South Carolina and a graduate of University of South Carolina, where he pursued classical studies and law. He was admitted to the bar in Louisiana in 1844 and practiced intermittently throughout his political career, first as mayor and then in national office.[93]

Landrum's success in city government, along with his personal record of achievement and reputation, led to his election as a U.S. representative in 1859 for Louisiana's Fourth Congressional District. Landrum was an example of a Southern Democrat on the eve of Civil War; his understanding of state sovereignty convinced him that secession was the only viable political alternative for Louisiana amid the brewing sectional tensions following the election of Abraham Lincoln in 1860. This put him squarely at the intersection of history, as Landrum was one of the southern delegates who left the floor of the House of Representatives in January 1861 when Louisiana joined the ranks of other seceded southern states.[94] Landrum's death in October 1861 meant that he did not see the conclusion of the historic events that unfolded while he was in Washington or in the years immediately following. His monument in Oakland Cemetery is a large obelisk-shaped stone, noting he was "aged about 42 years" at the time of his death.

Albert Harris Leonard

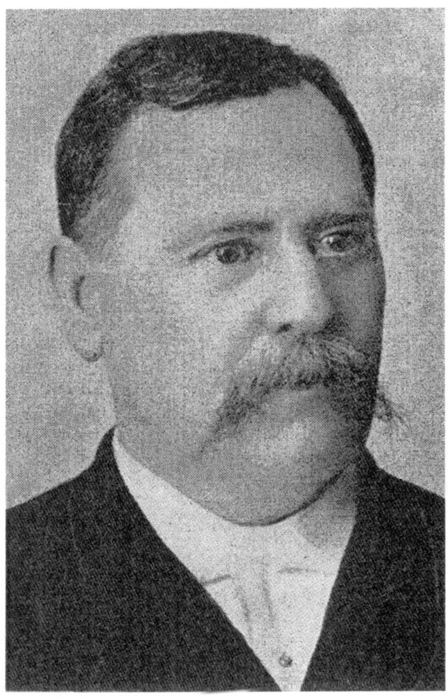

Albert Harris Leonard, the founder of the *Shreveport Times*. *Image from Lilla McLure and J. Ed Howe,* History of Shreveport and Shreveport Builders, *294.*

The son of a steamboat captain on the Red River, Albert Leonard was just a boy of ten when his family moved to Shreveport from Columbus, Georgia. Born in 1839, he was a true eyewitness to Shreveport's early identity as a river port and its defining moments during the Civil War, and his memoirs reflect his descriptions of a typical frontier town, complete with gunfights, dice games and nefarious characters.[95] His unique vantage point makes him an important and rich source of early city history.

With no formal education to speak of, Leonard nevertheless prepared himself for the study of law and was admitted to the bar at the young age of nineteen. However, when Civil War broke out in 1861, Leonard volunteered for service in the Confederate army (1st Louisiana

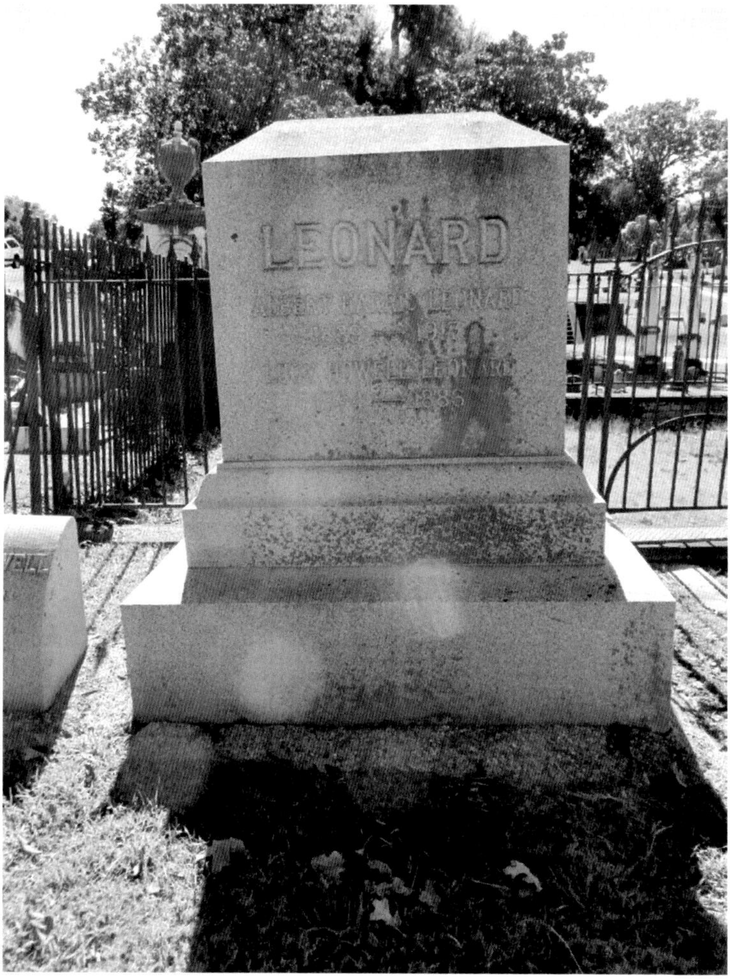

Albert Harris Leonard's monument lies near the east-center portion of Oakland. *Photograph by Gary D. Joiner.*

Infantry) before battle wounds in June 1862 resulted in a change of duties and an eventual honorable discharge from service.[96] He began practicing law in Shreveport in 1866 and, soon thereafter, was elected to the post of clerk for the District Court in Caddo Parish before entering private practice with Captain L.M. Nutt. Elected office continued to hold appeal to him, and he became a Louisiana state senator from 1872 to 1876. In 1877, he became the U.S. attorney for Louisiana and served in that position for twenty years before returning to the quieter life of private law practice. His final partnership was with E.H. Randolph and Allen Rendall.[97]

His domestic life included marriage to Lucy Howell in 1879, and the couple had one daughter, Cecelia Leonard Ellerbe. In addition to a life in law and politics, Leonard was also a successful farmer. He owned large amounts of acreage covering several Red River plantations and was an important figure in the early development of lands along the river for agricultural production. He was also one of the founders of the *Shreveport Times*, established in 1871, and is reported to have been responsible for bringing the first natural gas to Shreveport for use as a source of energy.[98] His imprint on the city is obvious even as it has expanded far from its boundaries of his own age; indeed, Leonard Road in southeast Shreveport was named in his honor.

His wife, Lucy, died as a young woman of twenty-seven in 1886, leaving Albert to care for the young Cecelia, age six. Cecelia grew up to marry Clarence Ellerbe (for whom another street in southeast Shreveport is named), and she became a widely published poet in addition to being one of the original founders of the Woman's Department Club. Cecelia was also instrumental in the early organizational structure of the Shreveport Little Theatre, which is now one of the oldest continuously operating community theaters in the United States. Albert Leonard lived until 1917. He is buried next to his wife, Lucy, in Oakland Cemetery, with a relatively simple monument marking their plot. Cecelia Leonard Ellerbe is buried in Shreveport's Greenwood Cemetery.

Captain Simon Levy Jr.

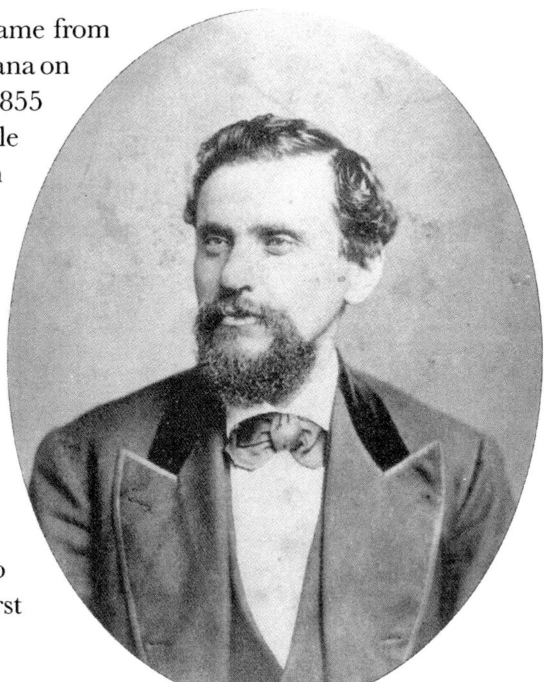

An image of Simon Levy Jr. as vice-president of the Kansas City Southern Railroad. *LSU Shreveport, Noel Memorial Archives.*

Captain Simon Levy Jr. came from Alsace, France, to Louisiana on the eve of the Civil War in 1855 and entered into the mercantile business in Shreveport with his brother, Samuel Levy (profiled separately herein). When war broke out, Simon enlisted in the Confederate army and rose to the rank of captain in the 1st Louisiana Special Battalion.[99] Following the war, Levy married Harriette Bodenheimer, the daughter of Jacob Bodenheimer, who was, perhaps, the area's first

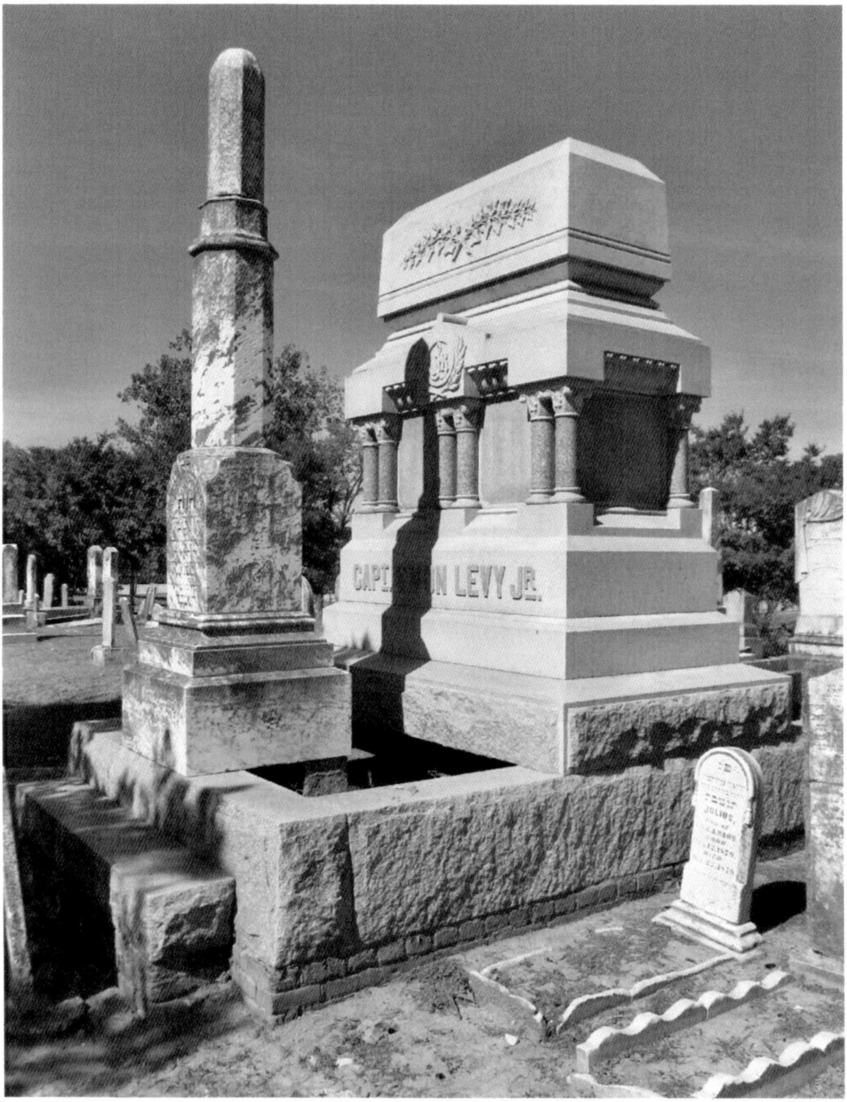

The monumental bedstead tomb of Simon Levy Jr. and his wife, Harriette Bodenheimer Levy, dwarfs all others in Oakland and perhaps the region as well. *Photograph by Gary D. Joiner.*

Jewish settler. In the 1870s, he owned a grocery store and a saloon with his brother-in-law, Lazarus Bodenheimer. Captain Levy was instrumental in helping to bond the early Jewish community of Shreveport, serving as president of B'nai Zion Temple from 1879 to 1881. He also owned and operated the Banking House, which was the forerunner of Commercial National Bank. Levy became that bank's first president, and CNB would enjoy a long history of success in Shreveport. He was also vice-president of Kansas City Southern Railroad and was an important advocate for its coming to Shreveport.[100]

The state of the railways in the area following the Civil War was understandably poor since much of the construction underway across the South connecting major cities had ceased when war broke out. Much of the rail that remained had been damaged. By 1897, Kansas City Southern had over five hundred miles of new track from Shreveport to St. Louis, and another major port on the Mississippi River was connected to Shreveport by rail.[101] Levy was instrumental in encouraging and promoting this economic development. The impact of the Levy brothers in helping to shape the economy of the area in the late nineteenth century cannot be understated, and Captain Levy's own business enterprises were great successes. He was a generous philanthropist and social activist, helping to establish the Louisiana Charity Hospital System and serving on that institution's first board of governors in 1876.[102]

When the Levy brothers arrived in Shreveport in the 1850s, the Jewish community was quite small in number. By 1861, the community adopted the name Har-el and met in local homes. By the end of the Civil War, the Jewish community became known as Hebrew Zion and began construction on its first house of worship on Fannin Street. Shortly thereafter, there was a split in the congregation over rival traditions of Judaism, but by 1877, the two Jewish groups had reconciled as part of the Reformed tradition. Levy did not live to see that congregation swell to outgrow its Fannin Street location, precipitating the construction of a new B'nai Zion temple at the corner of Common and Cotton Streets, but he was clearly influential in the years of its most rapid growth.[103]

Simon and Harriette Levy had no children, and theirs is a bizarre burial story at Oakland Cemetery. Harriette died in 1878 and Simon in 1898, but Harriette is actually buried atop her husband's grave. There was limited space in the Hebrew Rest portion of Oakland Cemetery, so she was exhumed to permit the burial of her husband and then was reinterred atop him. Their plot in Hebrew Rest is therefore one of the most interesting in all of Oakland Cemetery. Their tomb is also one of the most majestic. Technically a bedstead monument, resting atop the bed frame is a very large neoclassical stone accompanied by a column dedicated to Harriette.

Samuel Levy

The rise of Samuel Levy to prominence in Shreveport could hardly have had worse historical timing. As the first of Shreveport's four Jewish mayors, his life in public service was unfortunately intersected by the politics of the Reconstruction era and the yellow fever epidemic of 1873. Samuel Levy served in the 3rd Louisiana Cavalry.[104] Immediately following the Civil War, Levy served the city in its finance department. The Reconstruction governor of Louisiana from 1873 to 1877, the former Republican U.S. senator William Pitt Kellogg, appointed Dr. Joseph Taylor to the office of Shreveport mayor, and Levy continued to function within the city administration. However, by 1873, allegations of corruption within the Taylor government, resulting in the diversion of city funds for the personal benefit of Taylor and close associates, provoked the public to demand Taylor's resignation. He did so in August 1873, and Levy suddenly found himself as mayor until such time as the next election could be held later that same year.[105]

It could not have been a more challenging time for the city to find its coffers empty. Yellow fever struck Shreveport in the middle of August 1873, and within a brief period of weeks, the city lost one-fourth of its population to the illness.[106] With an economic crisis gripping the city due to Taylor's malfeasance and the great need for funds to combat the epidemic, Levy simply used his personal funds to pay the city's operating expenses. It was a measure that was not only extraordinary but also quite unprecedented. His tenure as mayor may have been brief, but his contributions to Shreveport during a time of significant challenge were remarkable.

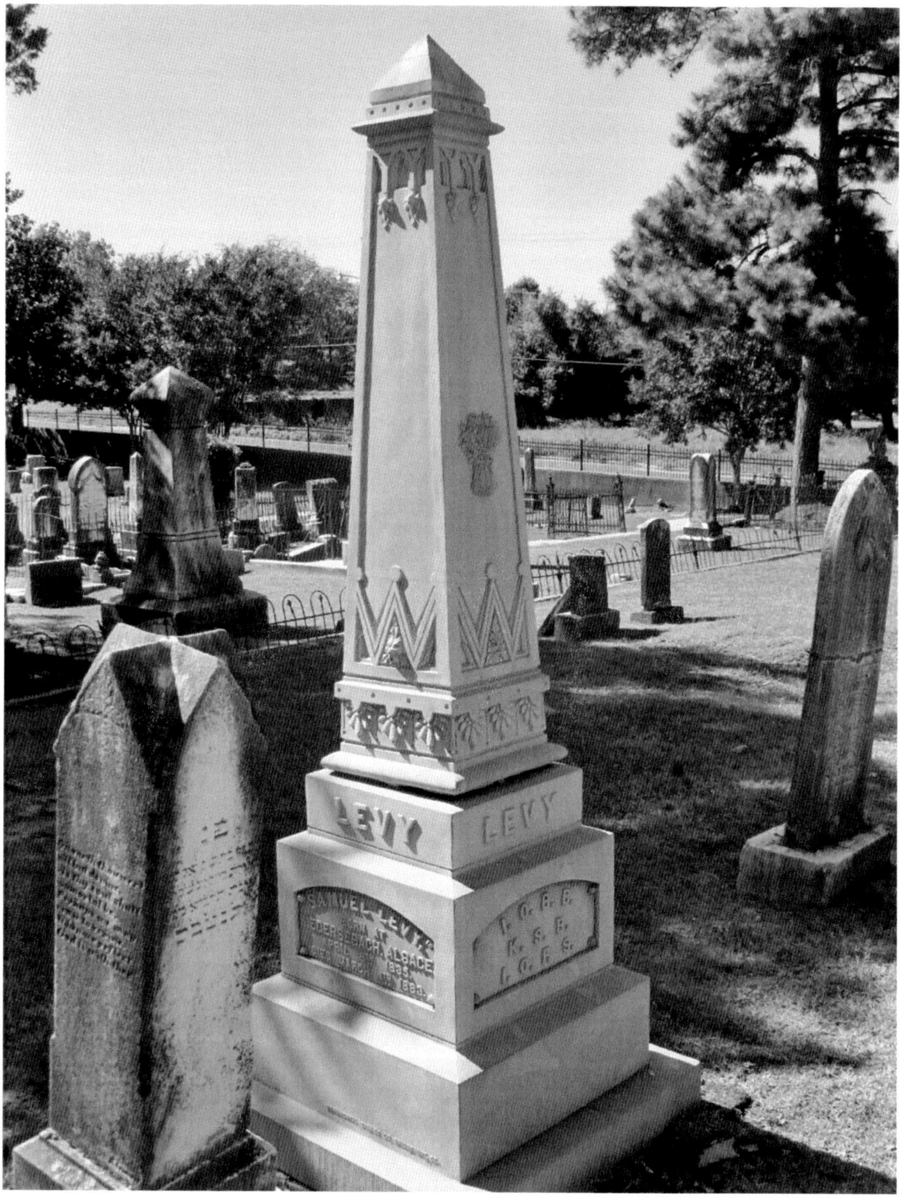

Samuel Levy's white bronze (zinc) monumental column is located adjacent to his wife's and his brother's (Simon Levy Jr.) monuments. *Photograph by Gary D. Joiner.*

Born in 1835 in Alsace, France, Levy came to the area at a time when many Jewish immigrants were settling in Shreveport, and he served in the Confederate army. Among Samuel's siblings, his brother Captain Simon

Levy also forged a successful life in Shreveport as one of the founders of the Kansas City Southern railroad and Commercial National Bank. Samuel Levy married a young widow named Louisa Stagleman, and the couple had seven children. Daughter Julia Levy died in 1881 at the age of fifteen, and son Moses Levy died in infancy in 1869. Those children are buried near their parents in the Hebrew Rest section of Oakland Cemetery. Louisa's grave is unmarked, but Samuel Levy's monument reflects an active life of community service. Levy belonged to several fraternal orders, including the Independent Order of B'nai B'rith, the Independent Order of the Free Sons of Judah and the Ancient Jewish Order of Kesher Shel Barzel.

Lafayette Robert Logan

A Confederate Colonel from Virginia serving with the 44th Tennessee Infantry Regiment,[107] Lafayette Robert Logan originally came to know this area because of his travels as a soldier, and he settled in Marshall, Texas, after the Civil War concluded. There he was a partner in a hardware store named Logan and Whaley until he moved to Shreveport in 1892.[108] Logan opened an icehouse and began brewing beer, establishing the Shreveport Ice and Brewing Company. In addition, Caddo Brewery, which Logan managed, became a subsidiary of Anheuser-Busch, brewing Caddo Beer and Budweiser, as well as a medicinal brand known as Shreveport Select Beer.[109] This would prove to be the business in which Logan made a considerable fortune. However, the Parish of Caddo passed an ordinance in 1908 that made it illegal to manufacture, sell or consume alcoholic beverages.[110] Since this ordinance was not repealed until the United States rejected Prohibition nearly a quarter of a century later, it is likely to have had a negative impact on Logan's finances. He continued to distribute ice, however, which was an important commodity in the days before electric refrigeration.

Logan was a prominent citizen of Shreveport and gave generously of his time to local civic pursuits, including organizations such as the Elks Club. His chief contribution to the city might have been the legacy of his home, however. His wife, Lavinia "Livvy" Seay Logan, inherited a plot of land on Christian Street in Shreveport, originally owned by her father, Judge William Austin Seay,[111] and the couple began construction on what would become

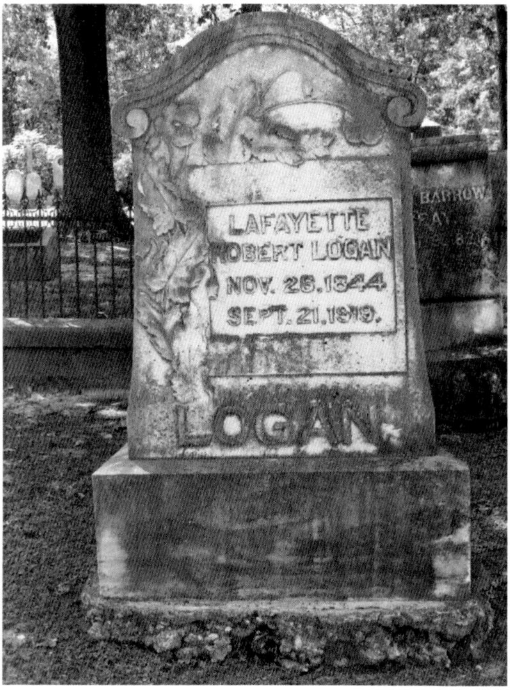

Left: Lafayette Robert Logan's monument is in the Seay lot. *Photograph by Gary D. Joiner.*

Below: Lafayette Robert Logan's mansion is located on Austin Place in Shreveport. *Photograph by Gary D. Joiner.*

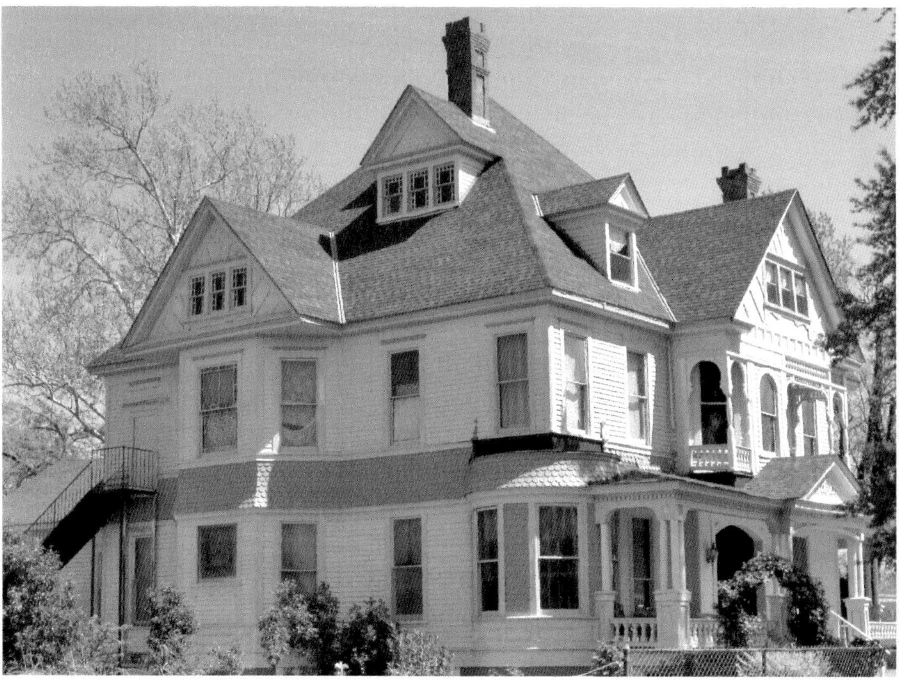

one of the city's most recognizable Queen Anne/Victorian–style mansions, which still stands.

The Logan Mansion was designed by noted architect Nathaniel Sykes Allen, and the cost of construction was around $15,000—notably opulent in an age when home construction averaged $2,000.[112] Upon Logan's death in 1919, the home passed to Wade Hampton, an executive with Kansas City Southern railway, and it remained in the Hampton family until 1955. The mansion has been home to churches and radio stations, but today it is owned by a local Shreveport couple, Billy and Vicki LeBrun, who have restored Logan's home to its original Gilded Age splendor.

Lafayette Robert Logan is buried at Oakland Cemetery near his wife, Livvy, and his in-laws, the Seays. From his grave can be seen the towering roofline of the magnificent home he built in 1897.

Colonel Leon Dawson Marks

A native of Bayou Sara, Louisiana, Leon Marks was a veteran of the Mexican War when he moved to Shreveport in the 1850s to open up a law practice. In 1859, he married Amelia Jordan, who was a relative by marriage of the future Union general and president Ulysses S. Grant. Marks also tried a career in journalism for a brief period of time, even publishing a weekly newspaper called the *Caddo News.*[113]

When sectional tensions in the United States began to build on the eve of the Civil War, Marks became one of the delegates to the Louisiana convention to decide the issue of secession from the Federal union. Marks was present following the vote counting on January 26, 1861, when the convention announced to the world that "the connection between the state of Louisiana and the Federal Union is dissolved; it is a free, sovereign, and independent power."[114] In the immediate aftermath, it was Marks who helped form the first infantry company (Company H) in Shreveport that would serve as part of the 1st Louisiana Infantry for the Confederate army. His last assignment was to the 27th Louisiana Infantry, which was fatefully dispatched to Vicksburg, Mississippi, just before the Union siege of that key Mississippi River fortress began. In the 27th Louisiana, Marks was promoted quickly through the officer ranks to colonel and was instrumental in overseeing the engineering design and construction of river defenses for Vicksburg. His promotion is noted in independent correspondence from Vicksburg, and it is clear that the men of his company admired and respected him.[115]

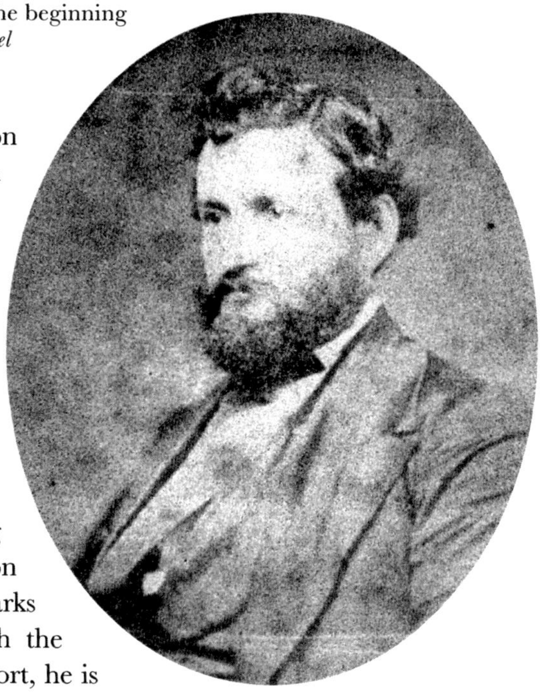

Image of Leon Dawson Marks at the beginning of the Civil War. *LSU Shreveport, Noel Memorial Archives.*

On June 28, 1863, a Union artillery shell exploded in midair over Colonel Marks as he sat quietly eating a meal. He suffered a serious head injury in the blast, and his family made arrangements to transport him back to Shreveport in hopes of a recovery. However, his condition continued to deteriorate after returning to Shreveport, and he died on September 23. Although Marks was Jewish and had ties with the Jewish community of Shreveport, he is

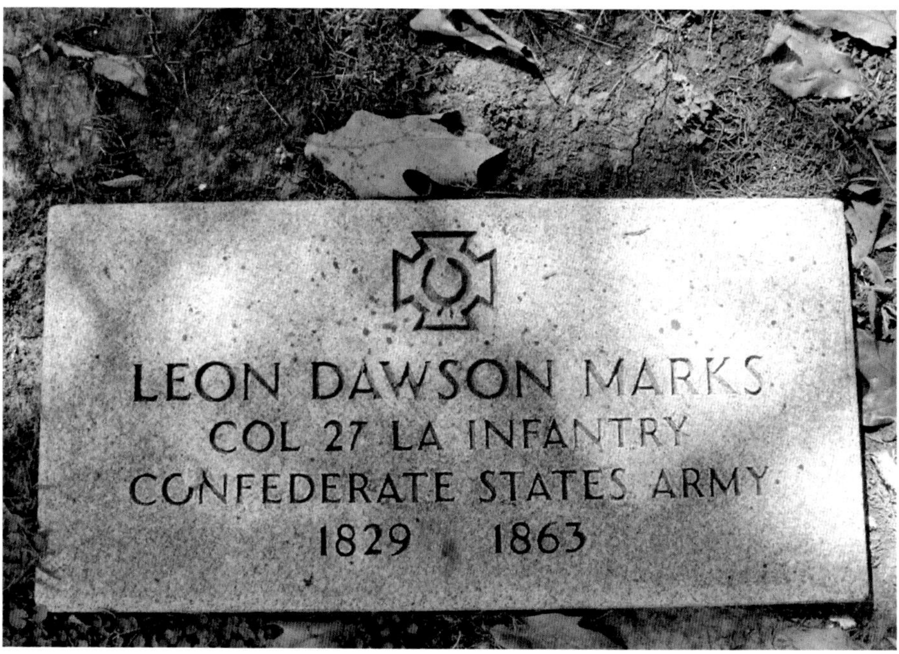

Leon Dawson Marks's military-style ground tablet marker. *Photograph by Gary D. Joiner.*

not buried in the Hebrew Rest section of Oakland Cemetery. His funeral was conducted with full military honors.

A tragic ending also awaited Marks's widow, Amelia, and their son, Francis. In 1869, they were aboard the steamboat *Mittie Stephens* when it sank in Caddo Lake. They both rest next to Colonel Marks in Oakland.

Annie McCune

Shreveport was home to a legal "red-light district" from 1903 to 1917, although prostitution certainly existed in the city from the time the first settlers came in the early nineteenth century. As a river city, Shreveport naturally attracted travelers and merchants, and even before the creation of a segregated red-light district, prostitution thrived on the riverfront of Shreveport in an area known as "the Batture," (or "river bed") located near the docks. In 1903, the Shreveport City Council established a legal district for prostitution in an area of the city known as St. Paul's Bottoms.

One woman especially emerged as the prototypical businesswoman of the era's illicit culture. Annie McCune has an iconic place in Shreveport history, known as simply "the Madam" and "the Queen of St. Paul's Bottoms." Although not much is known of her early years, McCune came to Shreveport during the Civil War, perhaps with Union troops up the Red River from New Orleans following the occupation of that city. Born in Ireland in 1840, her family may have been among the large numbers of Irish immigrants who sought refuge in America during the potato famines of the mid-nineteenth century. She may have resorted to prostitution as a means of survival.[116]

Historical records of Annie McCune's influence in Shreveport are somewhat scarce. A biographical framework within city history can be constructed from building deeds and other public records, but much of her personal life and story is unknown. Her first address within the city was listed on Common Street in downtown, and at least one brush with

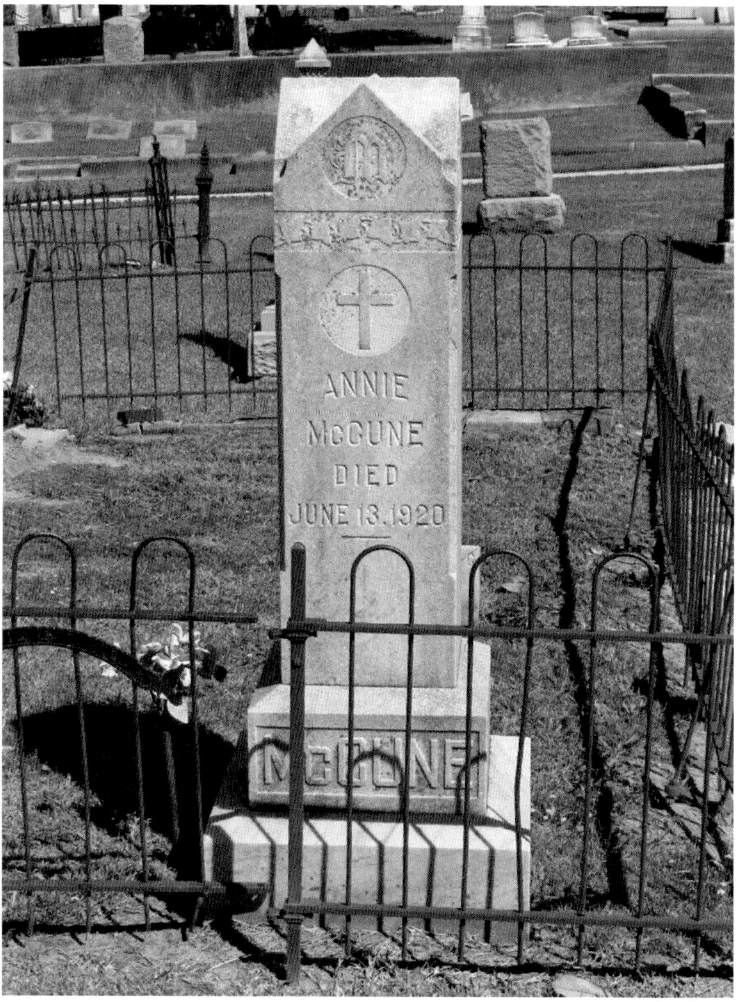

Annie McCune's cruciform column is one of the most visited sites in Oakland. *Photograph by Gary D. Joiner.*

the law was recorded early on—in the 1870s, she was arrested and fined for "streetwalking." Through legend and popularized myth surrounding her, there emerges an image of a kind but pragmatic businesswoman who cared for her women and her community. A persistent legend continues to posit that Annie McCune opened her house of ill repute as a hospital to victims of the city's yellow fever epidemic and that she herself nursed the ill and dying.[117] The 1900 U.S. census lists her as the head of her household, with an occupation as a "hotel keeper." Living with her at the time were two young female "boarders" with occupations listed as "seamstress" and "dressmaker."[118]

No longer in existence today, McCune's home was located on Cane Street (today known as Baker Street), facing the 900 block of Fannin Street near the edge of the district. It is unfortunate that due to the clandestine nature of the district and the very private lives of the women who populated those streets and buildings, historians lack details of life there. Annie McCune remains the most intriguing historical figure of this chapter of Shreveport history, yet much about her remains a mystery. There are no surviving portraits of her known to exist, and details of her private life are drawn from only a few public records. McCune married B.C. Secord in 1901 but then filed for divorce a year later when Secord abandoned her and left her with a diamond engagement ring that was yet to be paid for.[119] In her plot at Oakland Cemetery, there is the grave of a four-year-old child named Ada Mary Carlile—born November 16, 1895, died April 12, 1900. The date makes it unlikely that this was Annie's child; it may have been the child of a prostitute she employed. Annie was known to be generous of heart as well as a successful businesswoman. She died in 1920 from complications of diabetes, and her grave at Oakland is one of the most visited. Periodically, someone still leaves fresh flowers, usually red roses, there in memoriam.

Reuben Neil McKellar

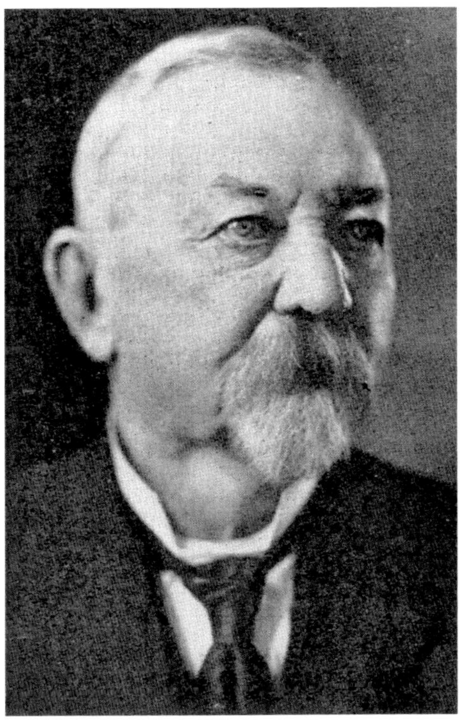

This image of Reuben McKellar is from a montage of early Shreveport mayors. *LSU Shreveport, Noel Memorial Archives.*

Known affectionately as "Uncle Rube" to the citizens of Shreveport, this city councilman, mayor, commissioner and community servant deserves the credit he has historically received for literally lifting the city out of the mud. Serving on the city council before being elected mayor in 1896 and later commissioner of streets and parks in 1922, McKellar was responsible for an ambitious and aggressive paving program for city streets, in addition to other important public works improvements. His contributions to city infrastructure, so vital to continued growth at the turn of the twentieth century, were quite significant.

McKellar was born in Kickapoo, Texas, and came to Shreveport as a teenager. His father was a cotton

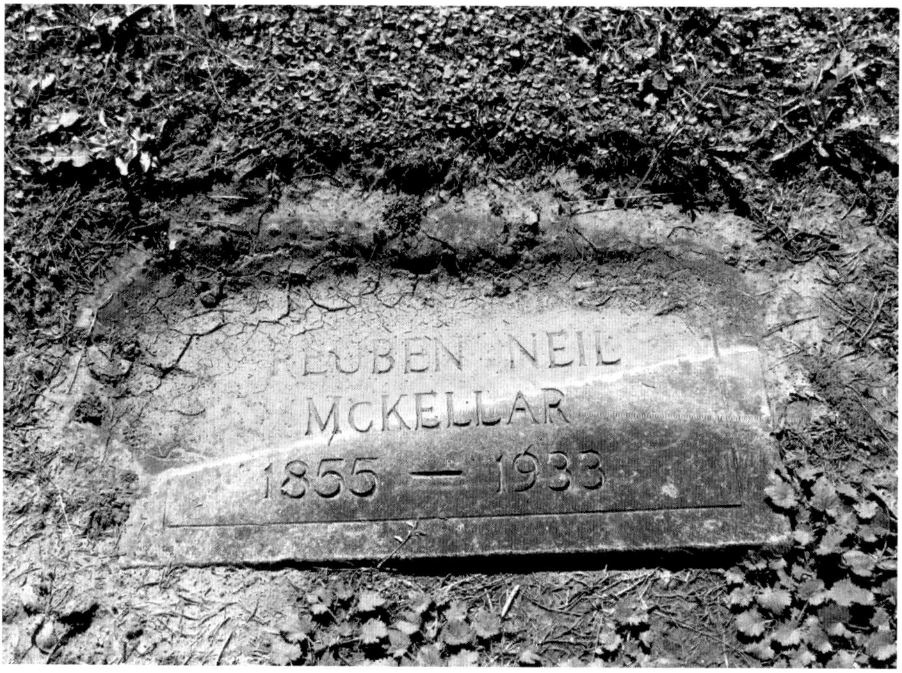

Reuben McKellar's simple ground tablet marker, near the Jacobs lot, is difficult to find. *Photograph by Gary D. Joiner.*

broker and built a business in Shreveport that McKellar continued after his father's death, even serving as president of the local cotton exchange in the 1880s. He married Theo Hamilton, and the couple had three children: Edwin, Mary Belle and infant Hamilton McKellar, who died at one month old. Their infant child is also buried in Oakland, memorialized with a marker that says, "Tiny Hamilton McKellar." The family made their home in an impressive Victorian structure on Oakland Street that still stands but is today an unoccupied and endangered historic site. McKellar's reputation as an advocate for public works improvements actually began while he served as a Shreveport judge; he was known to routinely sentence offenders with a fine of "$7.50 or 1,000 bricks." McKellar thought the fine of $7.50 sufficient for most misdemeanor offenses, and those offenders unable to pay were sentenced to lay one thousand bricks on downtown streets.[120] The impact that this modernization had on transport and commerce cannot be overstated.

Beginning with the first brick laid on Milam Street in January 1897, McKellar supervised the transformation of downtown from mud streets to the brick pavers that are the foundation of some of the downtown streets today. The work was extended to Texas Street and south to Jordan Street, with work completed by 1920.[121] Therefore, in every sense of the word, McKellar was a true builder of Shreveport. His interest in city improvements also extended beyond elected public service. While mayor, he supervised the first sewer completion on Texas Street and the building of Princess Park. However, after he left the mayor's office, he continued to work in private construction to build sidewalks and pave alleys throughout downtown. McKellar is also responsible for the entrance gate to Fort Humbug, which still stands today.[122]

Like many civic-minded men of the early twentieth century, McKellar served in several community and fraternal organizations. In addition to public office, he served as a director of the Commercial National Bank and was a member of the fraternal order of the Knights Templar and the Shreveport Elks Club. Reuben McKellar died on May 12, 1933, and funeral services were held at his Oakland Street home. His final resting place is a family plot shared with wife Theo and "Tiny Hamilton," as well as with daughter Mary Belle, who lived in Shreveport until her death in 1941.

James V. Nolan

A native of New Orleans born in January 1844, James V. Nolan matured into young adulthood just as the Civil War broke out. He entered the service of the Confederate States of America in 1862 at the age of eighteen, and he was attached to the 18th Louisiana Infantry Regiment.[123] He saw action at the Battle of the Mansfield during the Red River Campaign of 1864 as Union forces advanced toward Shreveport. Following his service there, Private Nolan was transferred to Meridian, Mississippi, under General Richard Taylor, where he remained until the Confederate surrender in April 1865. Like many other men fortunate enough to have survived the war, Nolan simply returned to his home and resumed his civilian life.

His father, James P. Nolan, had been a successful merchant before the war broke out and then served as a tax collector for the Confederate government in New Orleans until its occupation by Union forces in 1862. The New Orleans that Private Nolan returned to after the war was bustling with renewed prosperity. He began working for the Southern Express Company in 1865 and moved to Shreveport in 1867 as an expansion of that enterprise to the northern part of the state. In 1869, he married Jennie Bond, a native of England, and together they had three children. The family plot at Oakland is testimony to a stark reality in the nineteenth century—childhood mortality. There are found the graves of two of his children, both of whom died very young. Jimmie Nolan was stillborn in September 1871 and his sibling, Willie Nolan, died in 1876 at the age of four. The monuments for the children are not only poignant but also reflect typical iconography of the age. "Little

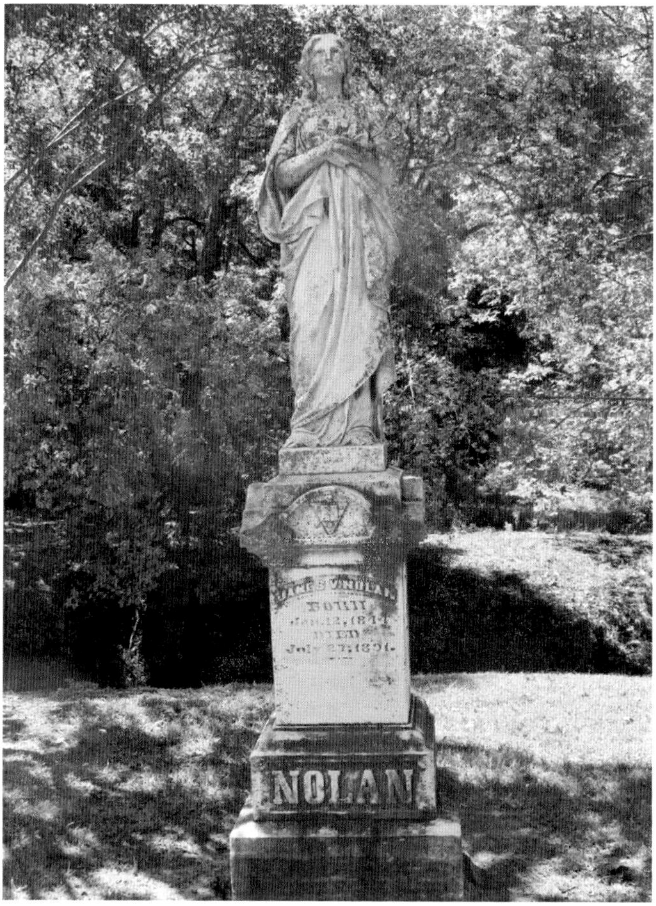

James V. Nolan's statuary column was carved by William Kinney. *Photograph by Gary D. Joiner.*

Jimmie" and "Willie" are memorialized together at Oakland with a shared monument. Jimmie Nolan's inscription reads, "Our little man," and beneath Willie Nolan's name are clearly the words of grieving parents, "Jesus took them in his arms and blessed them."

James Nolan's contributions to the social and civic life of the city are well documented in local histories. Besides becoming secretary of the local Cotton Exchange, he also was a charter member and vice-president of the United Confederate Veterans Association. He was a prominent member of Shreveport society until his death in 1891.[124] His monument in Oakland honors his membership in the secret societies (fraternal orders) quite popular in the nineteenth century. He was a member of the Knights of Honor, established in 1873 and dedicated to the principle of charity, and the Knights of Pythias, an 1864 fraternal order dedicated to friendship, benevolence and charity.

Genevieve Penick

The short life and tragic end of this little girl inspired a long-lasting institution that would honor the children of Shreveport in a quite remarkable way. Genevieve Penick, born in 1883, was the daughter of William and Bettie Penick of Shreveport. William Penick was the pastor of First Baptist Church. Just six years old at the time of her death, Genevieve choked on a glass eye that had been attached to a baby doll with which she had been playing.

Stricken with grief, her father decided to honor her brief life by establishing a permanent orphanage in her name to further honor efforts that were already underway. Tradition holds that just months before Genevieve's death, Reverend Penick had been profoundly moved by the sight of a homeless child whom he saw in the cold months of winter. An early chronicle of Shreveport quoted Reverend Penick as saying, "Sitting in my study one rainy night in February, I heard a gentle knocking and on opening the door, there stood a little girl with tangled hair, thinly clad and shivering with cold."[125] Immediately thereafter, he approached the wealthy widow of prominent Shreveporter Edward Jacobs, Palestine, to help with funding a home for such children. Palestine Jacobs agreed to help and generously added her personal funding to the orphanage for nearly three decades. Penick then rented a home on Texas Avenue as a temporary location, and the city's first orphanage was established. Genevieve Penick enjoyed playing with the children at the orphanage and spent much time there herself until her untimely death just a few months later.[126]

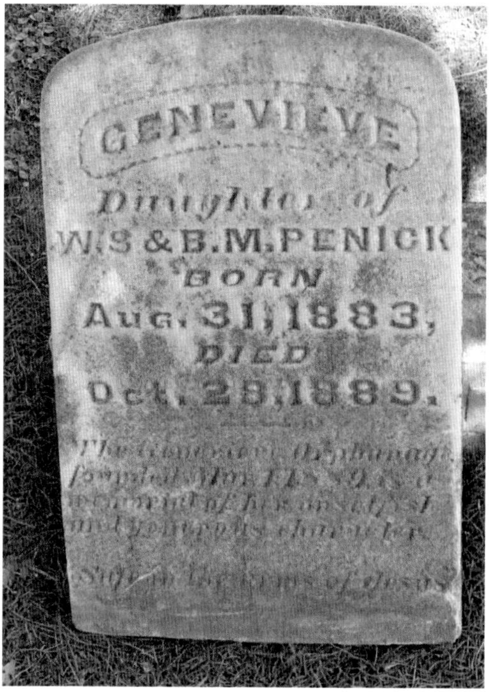

Genevieve Penick's marker is located in her family plot at its southern edge. *Photograph by Gary D. Joiner.*

The permanent structure that became Genevieve Orphanage stood on Olive Street, between Elizabeth and Warrington Streets, until 1962. The original structure that was dedicated in 1901 burned a few years later, so a second building was constructed in 1909. The idea of an orphanage as a response to the needs of homeless children was one that grew only gradually as the city of Shreveport grew and attracted a larger population. With the swell of city growth at the turn of the twentieth century, temporary measures no longer sufficed. The Genevieve Orphanage was both a necessary Shreveport institution and a city landmark; its services rivaled those to be

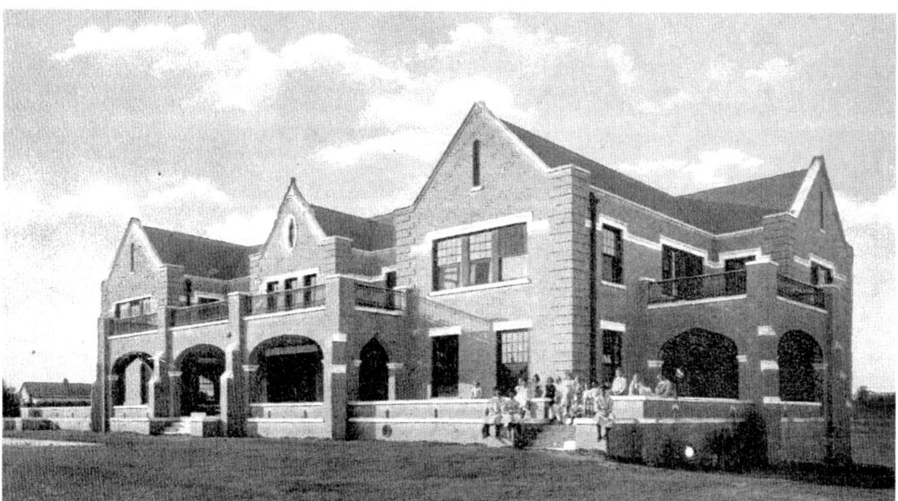

Postcard image of the Genevieve Orphanage. *Collection of Gary D. Joiner.*

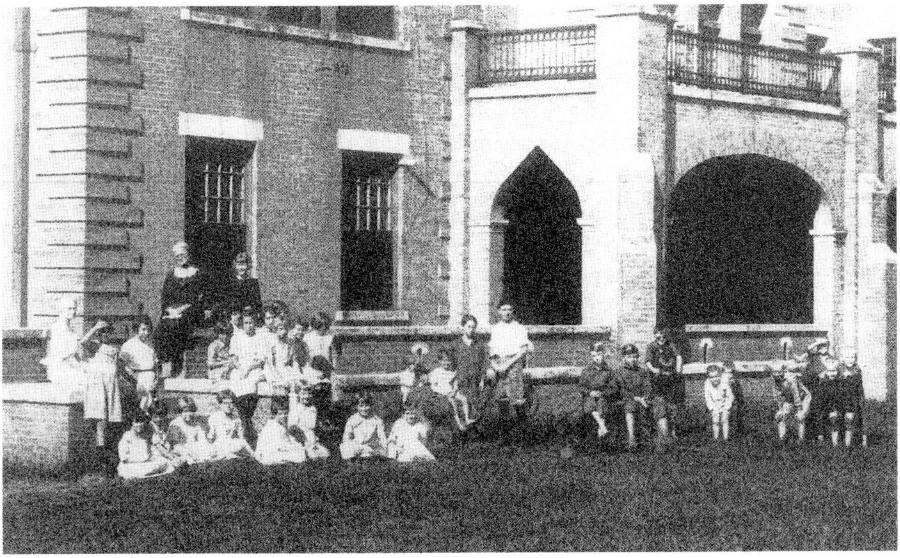

This photograph (date unknown) of the Genevieve Orphanage pictures some of the staff and children. *LSU Shreveport, Noel Memorial Archives.*

found in any city of comparable size or even larger. Social reforms of the mid-twentieth century brought new means of dealing with homeless children and orphans through the development of state foster care and adoption systems. The old Genevieve Orphanage became the Family Counseling and Children's Services Center.[127] Many in Shreveport still refer to the site as "the Genevieve," reflecting a fitting tribute to a child lost too young and her father's efforts to respond to children in need.

The grave of tiny Genevieve Penick in Oakland Cemetery is appropriately inscribed with the words of a father who responded to an acute personal loss by giving to others, "The Genevieve Orphanage founded in 1889 is a memorial of her unselfish and generous character. Safe in the arms of Jesus."

Julia Sparke Rule

As a woman who vigorously pursued a career as a writer for the *Shreveport Times*, Julia Sparke Rule was a true pioneer in a field that was almost exclusively restricted to men. She was, according to sources during her lifetime and shortly thereafter, the best-known female writer in northern Louisiana at the time.[128] Journalism in the nineteenth century was a man's domain, even for what might be considered "soft" news. However, this Shreveport woman defied the stereotype and, therefore, stands out as a remarkable exception. Born in Louisville, Kentucky, in 1851, Julia Sparke Rule belongs to an age that offered few career opportunities to women. Sadly, her life was marked by personal loss and tragedy, and she outlived both her husband and her son. She married Confederate war veteran Charles Rule, who died in 1881. The couple had one son, Glenn Rule, who died of a self-inflicted gunshot wound in 1911.[129] Yet Julia continued to work energetically until her own death twenty years later. In addition to her dedication to writing, Julia was also a gifted painter and artist.

Beginning as a reporter for the *Shreveport Caucasian* and later for the *Shreveport Times* and *Shreveport Journal*, Rule covered a variety of news topics. Unfortunately, because the news standards of the day did not always produce bylines for articles, it is difficult to know much about which pieces she actually wrote. However, Rule was responsible for beginning the society page, and here she wrote under the pseudonym "Miss Pansy." Under this pen name, Rule offered advice on everything from current fashion to social trends, noting significant community events and those in attendance. She

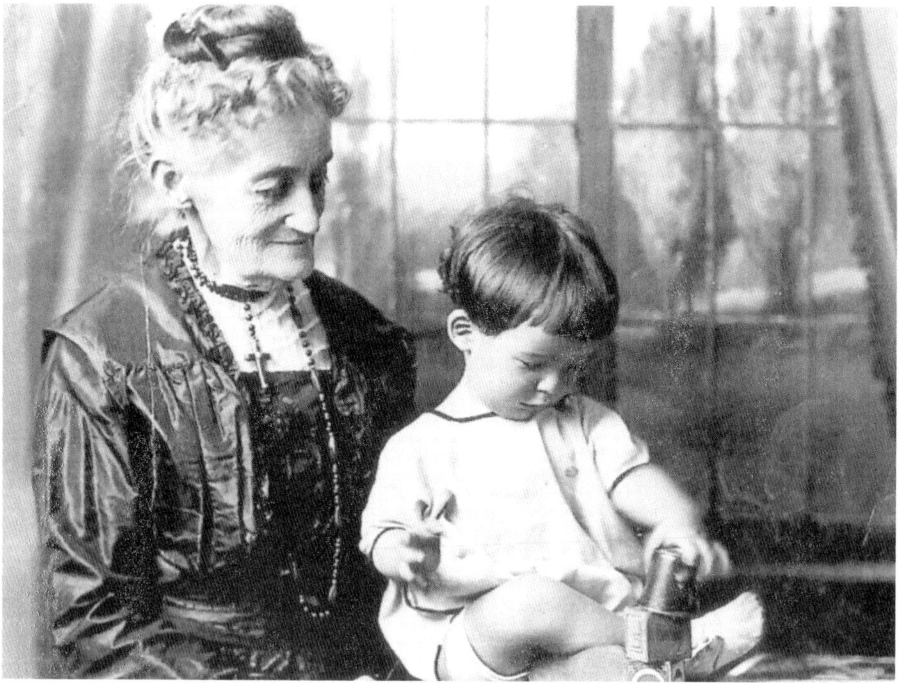

A late-in-life photograph of Julia Sparke Rule. *Collection of Anna Maria Sparke Keele.*

was part gossip columnist and part society editor but quite popular and widely read.

Julia had many interests outside journalism. She was also an advocate of physical education for both boys and girls. She taught calisthenics at the Kate P. Nelson Seminary—at the time, a prominent school for girls. As the State Fair of Louisiana grew in Shreveport, Julia became its first public relations director. She had a remarkable singing voice. A devoted member of First Baptist Church in Shreveport, she was reported to be the first person to have sung the hymn "Sweet Bye and Bye" in Shreveport.[130]

Julia Rule has the distinction of being the only woman to have been given the honor of driving a golden spike to mark the completion of a segment of railway. On April 6, 1888, Shreveport mayor Andrew Currie was slated for the honor of celebrating and marking the completion of the St. Louis and Southwestern Railroad, but at the last minute, he was unable to attend. Present at the festivities was reporter Julia Sparke Rule, who proudly completed the ceremonial task on the mayor's behalf. As the *Shreveport Times* reported at the time, she struck three blows to the golden spike while Reuben

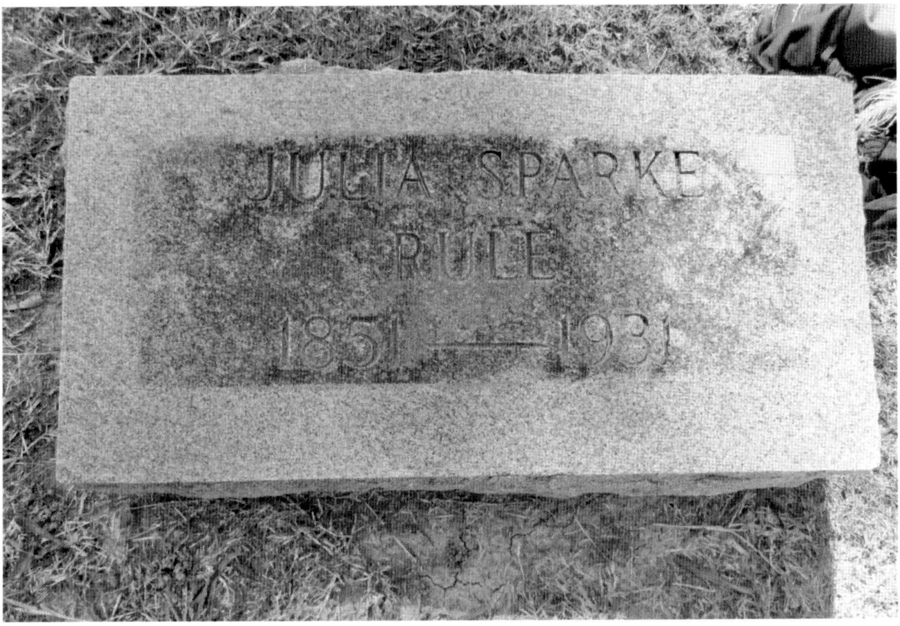

Julia Sparke Rule's ground tablet marker is found near the center of the cemetery on the western side. *Photograph by Gary D. Joiner.*

McKellar (detailed herein), who was at the time president of the Cotton Exchange, held it into position.[131]

Julia contributed articles for the local newspapers until just a few days before her death at age seventy-nine, on April 28, 1931.[132] As the *Shreveport Times* reported later, "The little, gray-haired lady that Shreveport honored and loved died and the entire city paid her tribute with respect and tears. Nearly everyone who knew her, and many did, called her 'Miss Pansy.'"[133] Her final resting place in Oakland Cemetery is notable for its simplicity with a minimal ground tablet marker that bears only her name and dates of birth and death.

Colonel William Rabun Shivers

William Rabun Shivers entered the pages of Shreveport history at a colorful and interesting time, for it was a period that witnessed three rival claimants to the office of mayor following a disputed 1871 election. The previous occupant of the mayor's office, Jerome Bonaparte Gilmore, decided to not seek reelection in 1871, leaving two candidates vying for the office—William Rabun Shivers and Moses Crowell. Shivers was a Georgia native who had served the Confederacy, reaching the rank of colonel in the 1st Louisiana Infantry as a member of the volunteer "Caddo Rifles."[134] The Caddo Rifles were organized in Shreveport in 1861, and records show that the volunteer group received

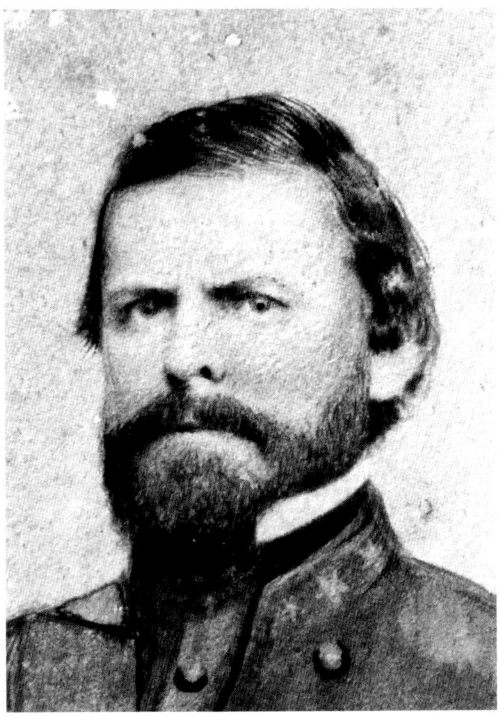

In this image of William R. Shivers, he poses in his confederate officer's uniform. *LSU Shreveport, Noel Memorial Archives.*

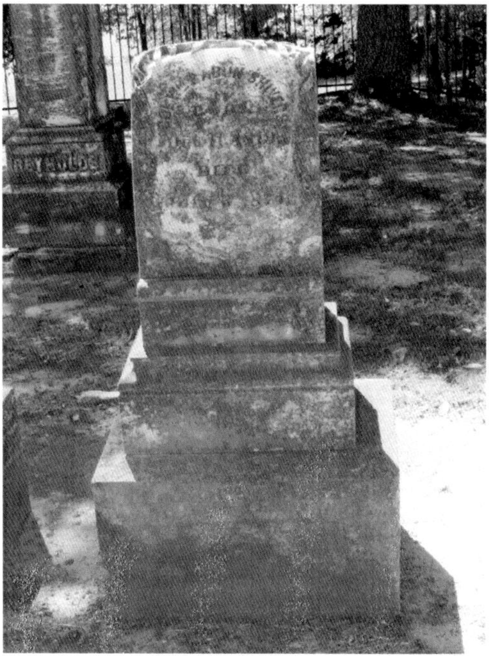

William R. Shivers's monument is found atop the western ridge in Oakland. *Photograph by Gary D. Joiner.*

a stipend of $4,500 payable to William Shivers as captain of the company.[135] In addition to being a veteran, Shivers also served on the Shreveport City Council from 1857 to 1858.[136] Shivers was man of considerable repute in the area, fondly remembered for his war service and leadership, a man who was at least twice wounded in battle.

On the other hand, Crowell was a Virginia native who achieved the rank of major in the U.S. Army and was commander of a corps of Union troops dispatched to Louisiana as an occupation force. Given the Reconstruction politics that prevailed at the time, Crowell was unpopular with most Shreveport citizens, but the election nevertheless proved to be close. The official vote count had Shivers winning by 24—371 to 347.[137]

However, the Louisiana legislature passed a bill during the summer of 1871 that permitted the governor to appoint city officials in lieu of elections. This was perhaps an attempt to cool tensions related to federal occupation during Reconstruction, but more likely, it was a ploy to gain and retain Republican control of the former Confederate state. It meant near chaos for the city. As it turns out, Governor Henry Clay Warmoth's choice for Shreveport mayor was Moses Crowell, not the local favorite, William Shivers. The dilemma resulted in a lawsuit in the Tenth Judicial District Court to resolve the three-mayor dilemma, but before those proceedings could get underway, William Shivers died suddenly on July 3, 1871, at the age of fifty-two. This effectively ended the legal challenge.[138]

Shivers was married to Sallie Elizabeth Sarah Trabue of Missouri, and they may have had one child,[139] although the census records for the period do not list the family in Shreveport. Colonel Shivers rests in Oakland Cemetery beneath a worn marker that is barely legible today.

Richard and Zachary Taylor

In the spring of 1863, Shreveport became the capital of Confederate Louisiana as the state government fled advancing Union troops that occupied New Orleans, Baton Rouge and, finally, Opelousas. As the gateway to Texas and a central point of commercial and economic impact, the city expected to be the next target of a Union assault. Preparations to defend the city began in earnest, focusing on the construction of batteries and fortifications along the river. The direct attack on Shreveport never came, for Confederate armies succeeded in stopping the Union advance at the Battles of Mansfield and Pleasant Hill in April 1864.

The Union army that moved north toward Shreveport was under the command of General Nathaniel Banks, who was supported by the naval forces of Admiral David Porter in what is termed the Red River Campaign. The Trans-Mississippi Department of the Confederacy moved to Shreveport in preparation for a battle for the city, under the command of General Edmund Kirby Smith.

Many families fled south Louisiana ahead of General Banks and came to Shreveport during 1863–64, causing the city's population to nearly triple. Among that number were the wife and four children of General Richard Taylor, son of U.S. president Zachary Taylor and the commander of the District of Western Louisiana, which was headquartered in Opelousas. In Alexandria on April 25, 1863, Taylor put his family aboard a steamboat with many other refugees to go up river ahead of the conflict. All four of the Taylor children contracted scarlet fever while en route to Shreveport.

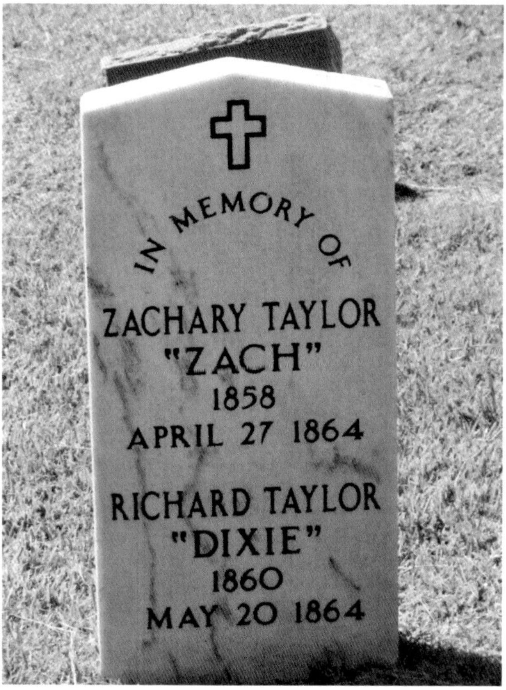

Richard and Zachary Taylor's military-style Confederate marker. *Photograph by Gary D. Joiner.*

Zachary Taylor, age five, died before reaching the city. His younger brother, Richard, lingered until May 20, just one month shy of his third birthday. The two older sisters, Louise and Betty, both recovered with no lingering ill effects.[140] The illness was quite common in winter and early spring and often reached epidemic proportions among combatants and civilians alike during the war, especially in crowded populations.[141]

It is a heartbreaking story that illustrates the precariousness of life in the nineteenth century, for scarlet fever is an illness easily treated today with modern antibiotics. General Edmund Kirby Smith arranged for the funerals of the children. The brothers are buried next to each other in Oakland Cemetery with a two-sided marker identifying them with names and dates on one side and inscriptions on the reverse that read, "Sons of Lt. General Richard Taylor" and "Grandsons of President Zachary Taylor." The exact location of the burials is unknown, but they are thought to be within the "Confederate Lot." The monument was erected by the Richard Taylor Camp No. 1308 of the Sons of Confederate Veterans.

Reverend George Tucker

A Tennessee native born in 1806, Reverend George Tucker came from a family heavily influenced by the period of revivalist preaching in America. His father, Jeremiah Tucker, was a Baptist preacher in Tennessee and Alabama throughout the early nineteenth century, and George followed in his father's footsteps. The family moved to Alabama in 1818, and all accounts indicate that they struggled with poverty, meaning that George probably did not receive much of a proper education. However, he was licensed as a Baptist preacher at the age of twenty-one, pastoring two separate Alabama churches, the Round Island Baptist Church and the Poplar Creek Church. He also married Rachel Hartsfield in 1827.[142]

By 1835, George and Rachel relocated to Columbus, Mississippi, which had only a limited and relatively disorganized Baptist presence in the state. George began building a congregation within that small community, briefly using even the basement of a local courthouse as a church. From there, Reverend Tucker moved back to Tennessee briefly and then to Marshall and Houston, Texas, before finally arriving in Shreveport in 1861.[143] The year that the Civil War broke out, Reverend Tucker was the new pastor of the First Baptist Church in Shreveport and faced the dilemma of every able-bodied man of the era, but especially the clergy, of whether to take up arms and enlist in the fight.

Tucker entered the Confederate army in March 1862, serving in the "Caddo Confederates" of the 27th Louisiana Infantry, and reached the rank of major before his discharge.[144] Following the fall of Vicksburg, Mississippi,

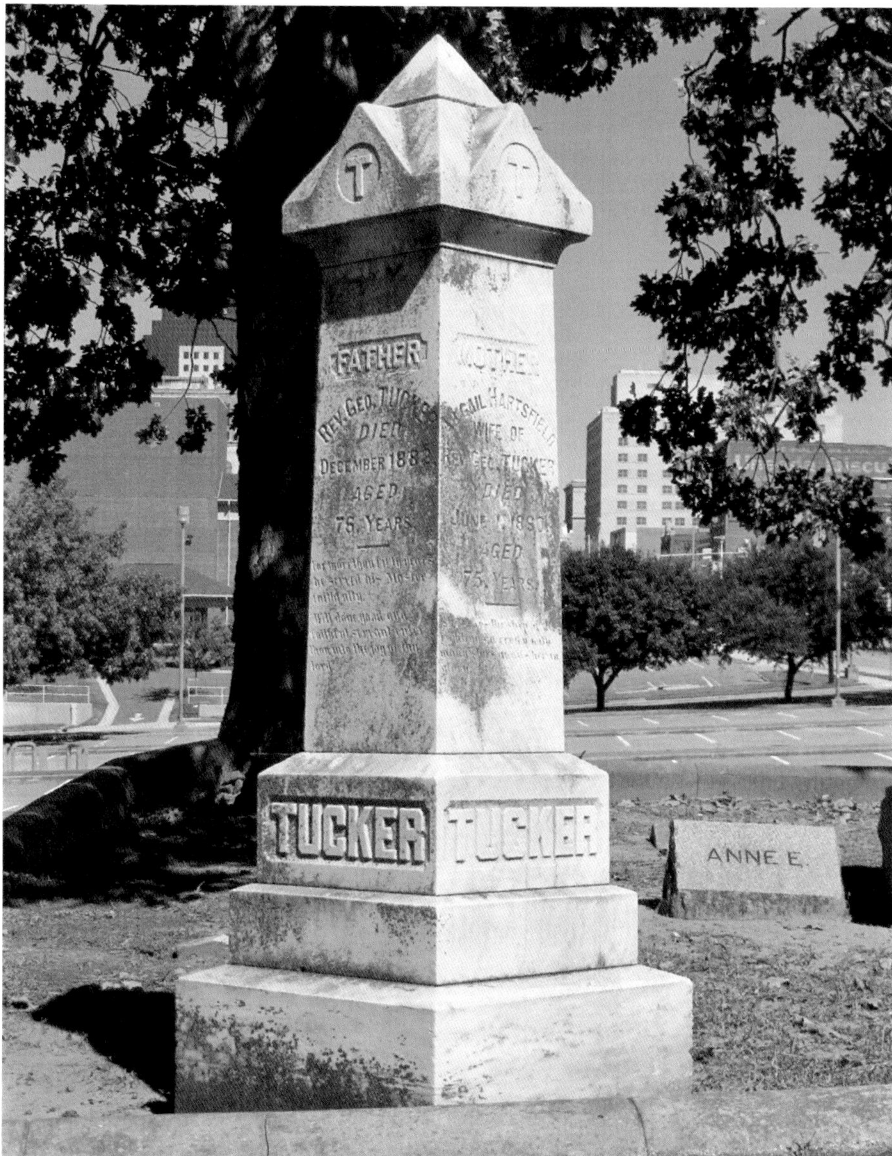

Reverend George Tucker's obelisk monument is ornamented with a capital *T* rather than the tradition Christian cross. *Photograph by Gary D. Joiner.*

where the 27th played an important role, Reverend Tucker returned to Shreveport. While preaching one Sunday, a member of Quantrill's Raiders rode on his horse into Baptist Church on Texas Street. Drunk and belligerent, he insulted the pastor's wife. The good reverend pulled out a pistol and shot the man in the chest and, supposedly, continued his sermon.[145] After the war's conclusion, Tucker moved his family to New Orleans, where he tried a career as a merchant, but this proved to be a failed venture. The Tuckers returned to the Shreveport area, settling near Keachi, Louisiana, where he continued to preach occasionally.

Tucker died in 1882 at the age of seventy-six, and his marker at Oakland Cemetery is affectionately titled, "Father," with an inscription below that says simply, "For more than fifty years, he served his Master faithfully." He and Rachel had three children. Sons Jeremiah and Andrew both also served in the 27th Louisiana Infantry. Their daughter, Harriet, is buried in Oakland Cemetery near her husband, George Turner, also a Confederate war veteran. Rachel Tucker died in 1890 and rests next to her husband.

Richard Tucker Vinson

Mayor of Shreveport from 1892 until 1896, Richard Tucker "Dick" Vinson is responsible for beginning some of the street improvements that his immediate successor, Rueben McKellar, would expand and continue. During his mayoral term, many of the main thoroughfares in the downtown area were substantially improved by the addition of gravel to dirt, and the heavily trafficked crossings received vitrified brick, which is brick that has been glazed to make it impervious to water. Because of this popular and noteworthy improvement of the time, Richard Vinson became affectionately known as "Vitrified Dick."[146]

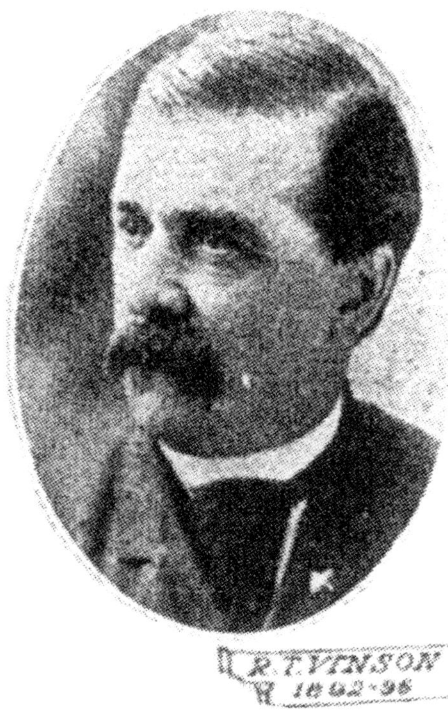

This image of Richard T. Vinson is from a montage of early Shreveport mayors. *LSU Shreveport, Noel Memorial Archives.*

Born to successful antebellum sugar planters, Vinson was a native of Assumption Parish and volunteered for the Confederacy

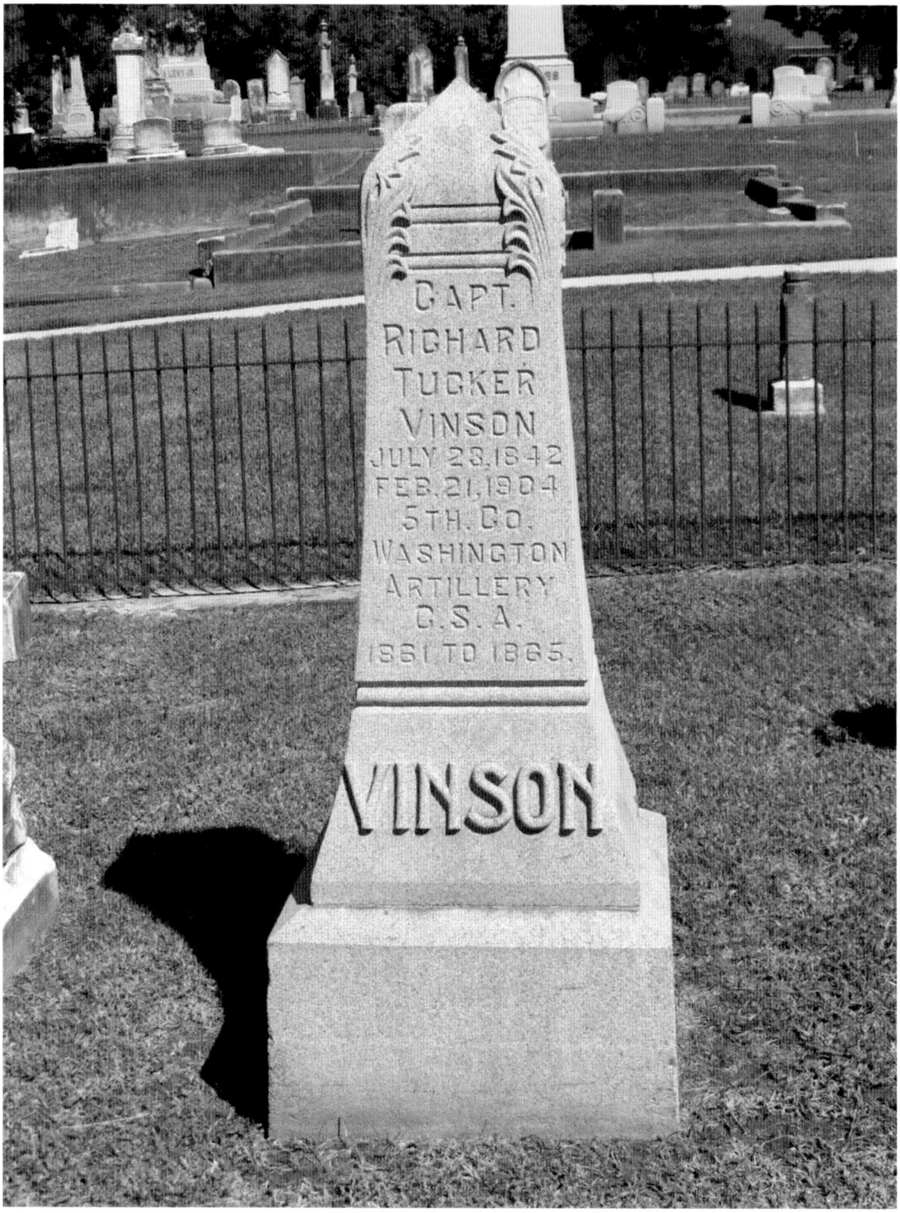

Richard T. Vinson's obelisk monument is found near the center of Oakland near Annie McCune's monument. *Photograph by Gary D. Joiner.*

while he was a college student. He quickly rose to the rank of captain despite a brief medical discharge due to measles, and upon reenlistment, he was transferred to the artillery division in Shreveport.[147] After the war, Vinson pursued farming in the area and began what would prove to be a lifelong interest in politics. In addition to serving as Shreveport mayor, he also served terms on both the Caddo and Bossier Police Juries.[148]

It was as Shreveport's mayor, however, that Vinson left his mark. In addition to the street improvements, his tenure also witnessed remarkable expansion of Shreveport's rail capacity, concluding with an agreement he reached with Kansas City Southern to construct rail lines into the city. It was also during Vinson's mayoral administration that the work was completed on the second Caddo Parish courthouse. Work began on the building in 1891 and was completed in 1896. It was located on the Texas Street site of the current 1928 structure.[149]

Vinson was married to Sallie Hill, a Tennessee native, and the couple had two children: Allen and Adah. Son Allen is buried in the family plot at Oakland, and daughter Adah is buried in a separate plot. After Vinson's death in 1904, Adah took up the cause of maintaining memorials within Oakland Cemetery for Confederate war veterans.

Colonel Samuel J. Ward

Born in Wales in 1834, Ward came as a young boy to Cape Girardeau, Missouri. He reached early adulthood during the outbreak of the Civil War, and although Missouri was a "border state" occupied quickly by Union forces, he enlisted in the Confederate army. Ward served as commander of the 8th Missouri Cavalry under General John S. Marmaduke in the Trans-Mississippi Department.[150] Throughout the conflict, he saw military action in Missouri, Arkansas, Tennessee and Louisiana before being released from service in Shreveport in 1865.

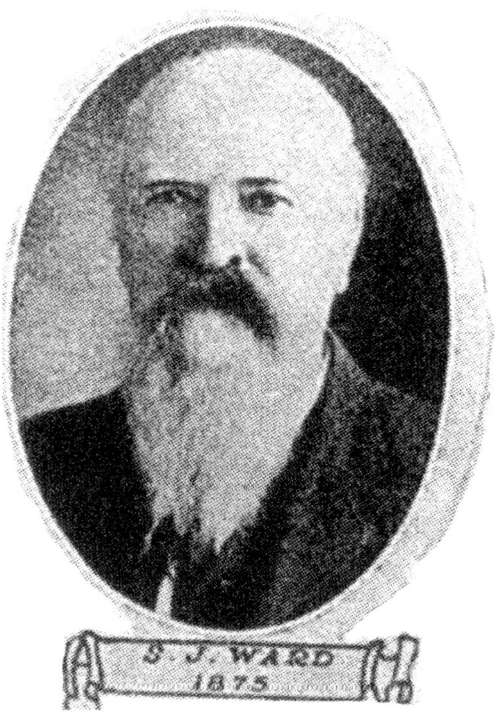

An image of Samuel J. Ward as an older politician. *Image from Lilla McLure and J. Ed Howe,* History of Shreveport and Shreveport Builders, *243.*

Ward remained in the area briefly following the war, long enough to marry Kate

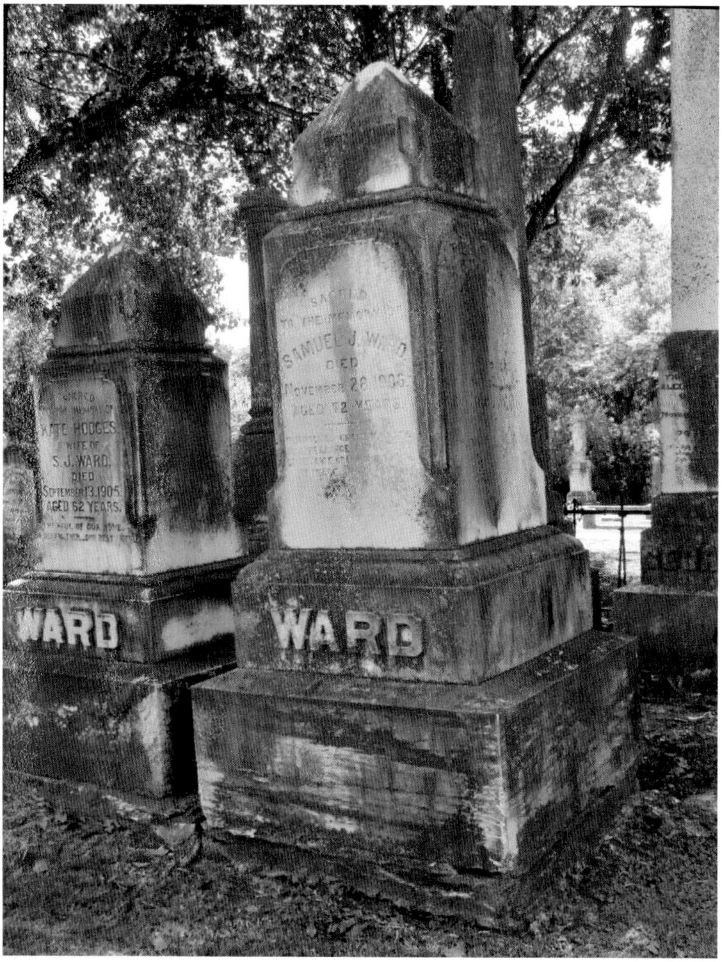

Samuel J. Ward's monument is within the Seay plot. *Photograph by Gary D. Joiner.*

Hodges from Bossier Parish, before moving back to Missouri, where the couple lived for several years. His return to Shreveport led him to follow his fellow Confederate veterans in joining the General Leroy Stafford Camp No. 3 of the United Confederate Veterans.[151] This was the third-oldest such organization in the South.

Ward's return was punctuated by his colorful and outspoken politics and a reactionary zeal to the presence of Reconstruction officials in the state. Besides being the first Democrat in an era of Republican Reconstruction to be elected mayor of Shreveport, he also served as sheriff of Caddo Parish from 1900 until his death in 1906. He is one of only a few men who served in both positions. His wife, Kate, predeceased him the year before.[152] During the turbulent years of Reconstruction, Louisiana was torn between the disenfranchised former Confederates, who were solidly Democrats, and the Republicans, who were black former slaves, carpetbaggers from the North and scalawags (southerners who cooperated with federal authorities). The Democrats elected Samuel Douglas McEnery for governor of Louisiana in 1872, but the federal army, under martial law, found the election illegal and voided the vote. For a brief period, Louisiana had two governors, two legislatures and two bureaucracies before the federal courts put an end to the situation.[153] Samuel Ward served as McEnery's adjutant general. He reprised this role during McEnery's administration from 1881 to 1888.[154]

The Wards had two sons, Samuel and Robert. The couple rest together at Oakland Cemetery.

Lieutenant Eugene Augustus Woodruff

One of the greatest heroes of the 1873 yellow fever epidemic in Shreveport was an Iowa native and Union army veteran who served as part of an operation to clear the remaining logjam on the Red River, an event that happened to coincide with the epidemic. Over the decades since the initial raft clearing completed by Captain Henry Miller Shreve, driftwood and debris had gradually filled up portions of the river channel, making steamboat travel a challenge by 1872. Lieutenant Eugene Augustus Woodruff of the U.S. Army Corps of Engineers came to Shreveport in 1872, when work commenced again on the river to clear remaining debris that was impeding commerce.[155]

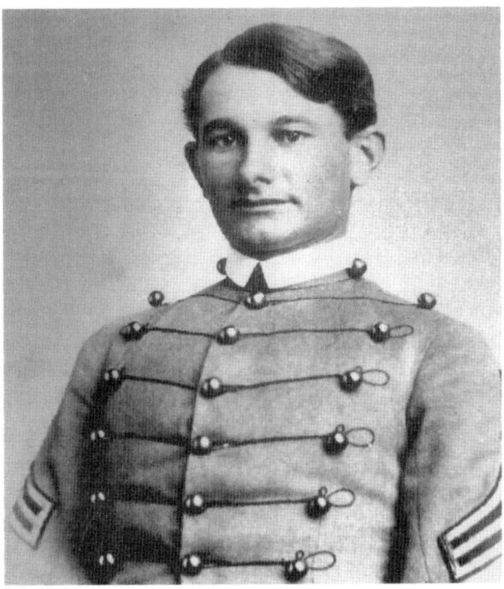

Eugene A. Woodruff is pictured here in his U.S. Military Academy at West Point senior portrait (1866). *LSU Shreveport, Noel Memorial Archives.*

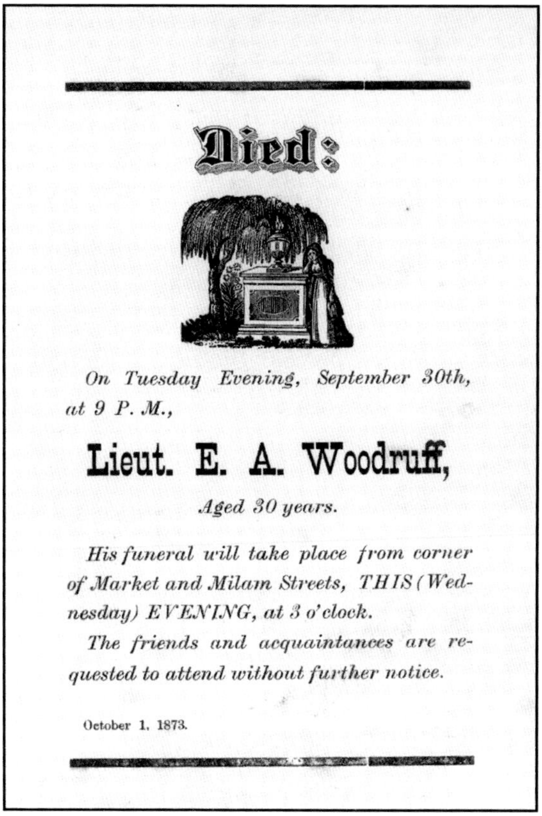

Died:

On Tuesday Evening, September 30th, at 9 P. M.,

Lieut. E. A. Woodruff,

Aged 30 years.

His funeral will take place from corner of Market and Milam Streets, THIS (Wednesday) EVENING, at 3 o'clock.

The friends and acquaintances are requested to attend without further notice.

October 1, 1873.

Eugene Woodruff's death card announces his funeral. *LSU Shreveport, Noel Memorial Archives.*

When the Civil War broke out, Woodruff entered the Union army, enlisting in July 1861 in Company E of the 5th Iowa Infantry, and reached the rank of corporal before he received the surprising news that he had been recommended to enter West Point Military Academy as a cadet. He graduated from West Point in 1866 and received a commission as a second lieutenant in the Army Corps of Engineers. The following year, he was promoted to the rank of lieutenant. Prior to receiving orders to report to Shreveport, Woodruff was stationed in Missouri, Wisconsin and Michigan. In 1871, he was tasked with making a survey of the obstructions on the Red River, and his report served as the basis for Congress appropriating the funding of $150,000.[156] From Lieutenant Woodruff's diary, historians are able to glean interesting details about not only the task facing the Army Corps of Engineers with regard to the Red River but also the yellow fever outbreak that was threatening Shreveport.

Lieutenant Woodruff noted that on Wednesday, September 10, 1873, he arrived for a midmorning meeting downtown, only to find people suddenly and seriously ill. He found the city in near chaos and immediately put himself in the service of the sick and dying. On the following day, he recounted that he went to Morris Drug Company to dispense medications for the sick because the epidemic had also claimed the local druggists. Woodruff was therefore also able to keep detailed records about the treatments being

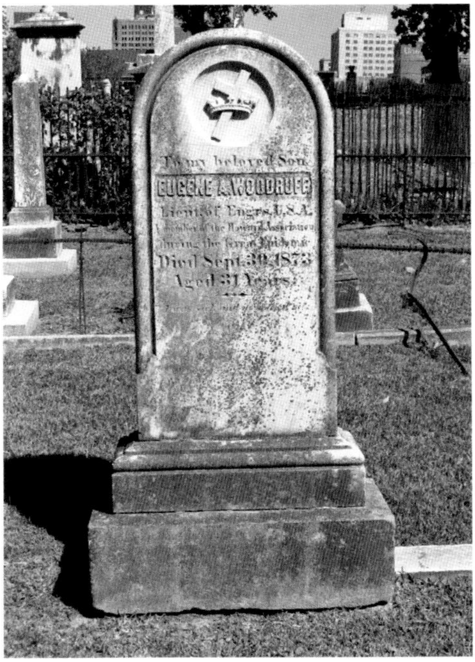

Eugene Woodruff's tombstone was carved in St. Louis, Missouri. *Photograph by Gary D. Joiner.*

used for yellow fever victims. The fact that he personally cared for sick strangers is documented in his diary. Woodruff made brief entries noting that for a period of about a week, he went with little sleep and with apparently little regard for his own safety. Although the Army Corps of Engineers ordered his detachment out of the city due to the epidemic, Woodruff chose to stay behind at the cost of his own life.[157]

Woodruff's story is remarkable and compelling. That a Union army veteran would be hailed a hero during Reconstruction in Louisiana was unlikely enough, but that such a man selflessly sacrificed his own health to care for strangers in an adopted city certainly warrants such commendation. Woodruff was buried in the Elstner family plot in Oakland Cemetery, donated by the family with whom he resided during his time in Shreveport. The city government drafted a special "Tribute of Respect" resolution to send to Woodruff's family, wherein it is noted that he "fell a victim to the dreadful scourge of Yellow Fever, while engaged in the Christian and philanthropic duty of attending to the afflicted and relieving the distressed."[158]

Yellow Fever Mound

In the summer of 1873, Shreveport experienced a horrific epidemic of yellow fever, as did other places throughout Louisiana. It was the worst epidemic the city ever experienced, even though yellow fever had visited twice before in previous decades. An estimated one-third of area residents may have fled Shreveport before the official quarantine became effective.[159] Early chroniclers and scientists have cited various causes as the origin of this particular infection, ranging from the wreck of a steamboat—the *Ruby*, which sank at the mouth of Cross Bayou while carrying one hundred head of cattle—to the introduction of the disease through a traveling circus company, "The Great James Robinson's Circus," from Mexico.[160] Immediately following the epidemic, medical attention focused on the city's apparently poor drainage systems and infamous lack of cleanliness. An official report written by a group of physicians shortly after the epidemic ceased noted, "The fact seems to be overlooked that this condition of this city has always existed, and while on general hygienic ground, want of cleanliness may foster and render more malignant the disease when once introduced, there is no evidence that filth and garbage…have ever, by themselves, generated yellow fever."[161]

Other theories of origin focused on the clearing of the Red River Raft. This theory was debunked because, of the estimated one hundred men employed during the season to continue to clear debris on the Red River, there was not a single reported case of yellow fever among them. The investigative committee concluded that the origin of the epidemic was importation from Cuba to New Orleans and then to Shreveport from the Red River. The committee also noted the disparity of racial infections, with whites affected mortally nearly six times as often as blacks, and that the greatest mortality occurred in men between the ages of twenty and thirty-five.[162] Why it affected the supposedly healthiest segment of the population most is unknown.

Yellow fever was a frequent annual summer visitor to Louisiana and claimed more than a few victims each season, but the 1873 outbreak was especially virulent. The port city of New Orleans suffered more often than most Louisiana locales due to the international contact of both humans and cargo. The riverboats were obvious means of transmission, but the railroads no doubt contributed to the spread of the pestilence during times of high infection rates.[163] Throughout the eighteenth and nineteenth centuries, Louisiana witnessed wave after wave of recurrences, so the scale of the Shreveport epidemic seems almost inevitable in this historical context.

In the early stages of yellow fever, the victim suffers with headache and fever, followed by a brief symptom-free period during which time a great number of victims spontaneously recover. However, many more progress to the third phase of the illness, known as the "intoxication" stage, in which organ failure begins to occur, progressing typically to delirium, coma and death. Medical science knows today that transmission occurs through Aedes mosquitoes and that it can be transmitted from infected humans back to a new mosquito host and then to another human, creating a cycle of perpetual infection.[164] This explains its prevalence during the summer months, particularly in southern and tropical climes.[165] Even today any resident of Shreveport can provide convincing testimony of the mosquito population during the hottest months of the year. A disease that is a cousin of yellow fever, West Nile virus, still exists in this region today.

One can only imagine the impact of the epidemic on the citizens of Shreveport, who most certainly reacted with disbelief and fear. The clergy were indispensable allies to the physicians in this tragic scenario, and in Shreveport, five Roman Catholic priests and two religious sisters heroically died in the service and care of the city's dying victims. Furthermore, many other local ministers and pastors remained and worked among the sick and dying, even opening up their churches to serve as hospitals. Another hero who succumbed to the fever was U.S. Army first lieutenant Eugene Augustus Woodruff, profiled separately herein, who was the commander of the U.S. Army Corps of Engineers unit tasked with clearing the Great Raft. The logjam had reappeared in 1872, and Congress wanted the Red River opened for commerce. Woodruff and his men had made great progress when the fever struck. The army ordered the unit to leave Shreveport for its own safety, but Woodruff remained to help the people of Shreveport in their time of need and succumbed himself to the illness.[166]

The epidemic in Shreveport and the ensuing application of drastic measures attracted national attention. The September 30, 1873 edition of the *New York Times* reported on the mass burials, with the following poignant update from a citizen witness: "Several of the most prominent and useful citizens of Shreveport have fallen victim to the epidemic...the population fearfully thinned out by sickness and death. We no longer have funerals."[167] The witness in this article noted that there were already four hundred dead in Shreveport, with another seven hundred or more infected and ill with the disease. The city seemingly shut down and stalled to a stop because of fear of the spread of the infection and a rapid loss of the supporting workforce. The witness made the following surreal description: "The hearses, followed by one or two carriages, dash through the streets like a section of artillery in a battle seeking a position."[168] Shreveport was quarantined by the federal authorities and by neighboring towns. The railroad was blocked to the west by Marshall, Texas, and on the east by Minden, Louisiana. The Red River was blocked by quarantine vessels.

There are several people buried in the Yellow Fever Mound at Oakland who did not die of the illness—or, at least, the initial diagnosis pointed to other causes. Two buried in the mound resulted from gunfire. The City of Shreveport sold lots on the edges of the mound several years after the epidemic.[169] The most unusual burial is that of Charles Pritchard, who was shot and killed while trying to enter and loot a mercantile on Texas Street during the epidemic.[170] It is likely that there are others who are buried within the mound whose stories are waiting to be revealed. Recent investigations used the daily death tallies combined with social and news columns in the *Shreveport Times* between August 15 and November 15, 1873, to achieve a total death count. Within Oakland Cemetery, 726 bodies were interred in the mound. An additional 78 yellow fever victims lie buried in Oakland Cemetery in family plots. During later decades, 13 people were reinterred in other cemeteries.[171]

Emergency public health measures were conducted by the Howard Association of New Orleans. This philanthropic group, which began in Liverpool, England, was re-created specifically to assist in yellow fever epidemics.[172] Its motto was "Unto the Least of These."[173] Its most notable member in Shreveport was Lieutenant Eugene Augustus Woodruff.

Following the epidemic, the Howards, as they were called, presented gold medals to seven women who cared for the sick and dying. The names of four are known today, and two of the medals still exist. The medal

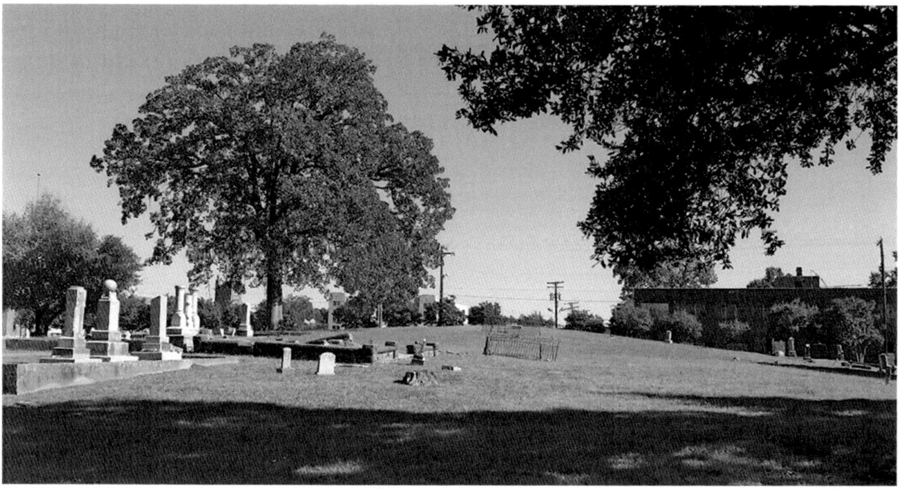

The Yellow Fever Mound today, facing south. *Photograph by Gary D. Joiner.*

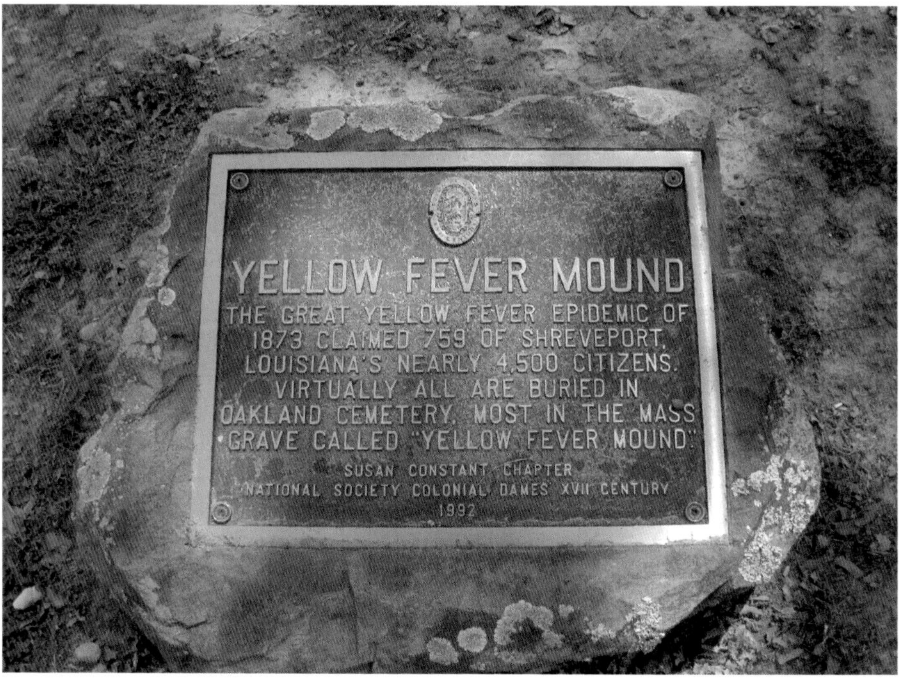

This bronze plaque marks the top of the Yellow Fever Mound. *Photograph by Gary D. Joiner.*

awarded to Florence Burkett remains in her family. Florence was the wife of Montfort Stokes Jones and daughter-in-law of Judge Roland Jones (profiled separately herein). These brave young women were justifiably referred to as "the Angels."

For more than a century, yellow fever turned up unexpectedly and stayed for varying periods of time but never with more startling ferocity than the summer of 1873. The disease entered the city's general awareness on or about August 27 of that year and continued until mid-November, a period of just over ten weeks of virulent infection.[174] At the end of the epidemic, which abated with as much mystery as it had arrived, Shreveport was left staggering at the cost. A single mass grave at Oakland Cemetery expresses the helplessness and inability of a city to deal with death on such a massive scale and illustrates a major turning point in the history of the city.

Below, left: Obverse, or front view, of Florence Burkett's "Angel of the Epidemic" medal. Of the seven awarded, only two are known to still exist. *Photograph by Gary D. Joiner.*

Below, right: Reverse of Florence Burkett's "Angel of the Epidemic" medal. *Photograph by Gary D. Joiner.*

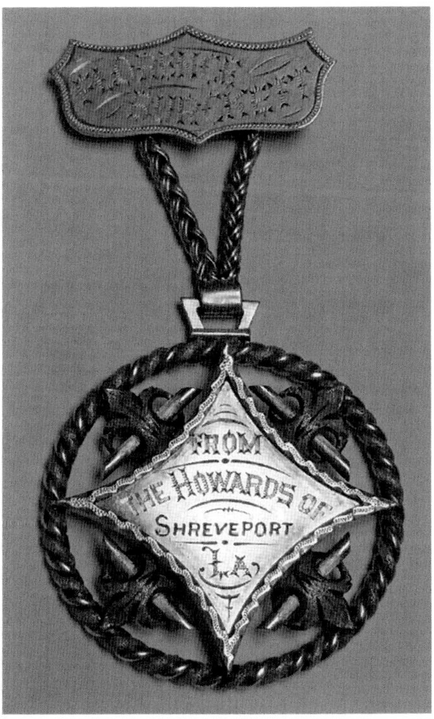

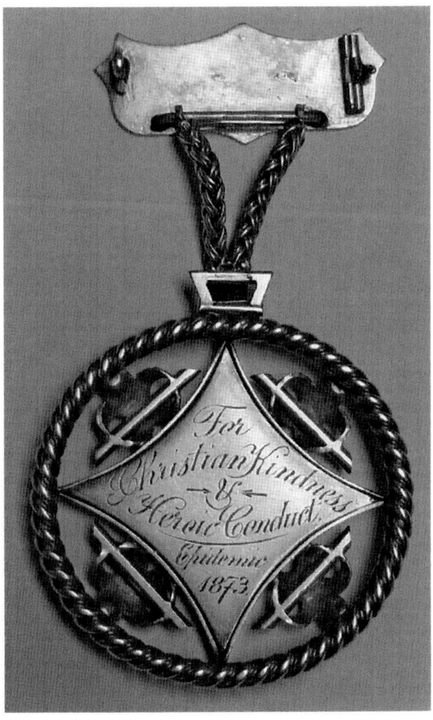

Appendix

Timeline of Significant Events in Historic Oakland Cemetery

The following excerpts from the city council records regarding the creation and maintenance of Oakland Cemetery demonstrate some important events in the life of this historic site, in addition to highlighting ongoing issues of concern that date to the cemetery's establishment. For example, early records indicate that there was a continuing need to address burials taking place outside of the designated cemetery, and several ordinances impose further fines and penalties for this. The city seemed keen to address, from the outset, the organization and order of the cemetery. Early trustees regulated by ordinance how individual burial plots would be maintained and segregated, which explains much of the wrought-iron enclosures and plot markers still visible in the cemetery today. Also, the abuse of pauper burials is a recurrent theme in the records, underscoring the large indigent population of the city and surrounding area in the late nineteenth century.

Interestingly, the issue of grave desecration and vandalism was one of the earliest to be addressed in the history of the cemetery, with the city even imposing twenty-four-hour imprisonment for those who defaced or disturbed this place of eternal rest. There appears to have been ongoing concern about the work of the cemetery sextons, preservation of the ground for future generations and reverence for stewardship and perpetual care. The occasional entry raises questions about what event might have precipitated the need for new city ordinances; for instance, an ordinance of 1861 requires that a sexton obtain certification of death from a physician or "three respectable citizens" concerning all deaths. One has to wonder if that is due to individuals being removed for burial who were not truly dead, as this was not altogether uncommon in the nineteenth century. Of course, the record entries during the fall of 1873, at the height of the city's yellow fever epidemic, are a poignant reminder of the crisis facing Shreveport.

An important part of Oakland Cemetery's place in history as the first and oldest city cemetery was the reality that the city would outgrow it; that its space would be depleted over time. The number of burials that cemetery sextons reported to the city government through the years is an important indicator of city growth, as well as times of public health concerns. Significant portions of the city government narrative address the challenges and delays in acquiring new dedicated lands for further burials. The city record also reflects conflicts over contracted work, most notably with regard to former mayor Rueben McKellar's construction of the now iconic and beautiful retaining wall around the cemetery grounds.

By the early twentieth century, the record shows increasing concerns about the deteriorating condition of the cemetery and its safety and security. This appendix lists the most significant matters in the city record through 1908. By this time, Shreveport had established Greenwood Cemetery, and Oakland Cemetery had truly become relegated to early city history.

(Excerpted from the minutes and records of the Shreveport City Council, except where otherwise noted.)

May 1846: The Trustees of Shreveport appointed a committee to find a "suitable burying ground" and report at a future meeting.

October 6, 1846: The city authorized the expenditure to purchase land for burials.

March 30, 1847: The Mayor and Trustees of the town of Shreveport have purchased the ten (10) acre lot known as Number Eighteen for burial ground for said town, with contract made by Lawrence Crain, Mayor, with Bennett & Cane:

1. All persons buried in town limits shall be buried in said burial ground.
2. Fine of $50 for burying anyone outside of burial ground without permission of the mayor and trustees.
3. Burial ground to be arranged in three divisions; one for a "Potters Field;" one to be under the control of the Mayor and Trustees; one to be subdivided into small plots and sold to individuals as private burial grounds.
4. The burial ground will be surveyed, with property divided into streets and enclosed, and the Mayor is authorized to sell lots twenty feet square for private burial grounds as soon as surveyed for the price of $10.00 each.
5. The mayor is authorized to sell the balance of said ten acre lot, in lots to said future purchasers.
6. Sexton for cemetery to be elected by a board whose duty will be the maintenance of the cemetery and to dig graves.
7. Sexton will be paid $50.00 per year and $5 for each grave dug, except for paupers' graves, for which he will receive $2.50.
8. Until the burial ground is surveyed, persons shall be buried on the hill in the southeast corner of the lot.
9. The mayor is authorized to draw on the city treasury for expenses in burying paupers.
10. The contract made by Lawrence Crain, mayor, with Bennett & Cane for the purchase of the lot for a burial ground was approved and entered into the record.

May 11, 1847: The Sexton is "required to keep a suitable hearse and horse." The Sexton is subject to a fine of $20 for every refusal or neglect to dig a grave, furnish hearse and horse for the use of persons applying, or to bury paupers on the order of the city.

July 23, 1847: An Ordinance Relating to the Burying of the Dead and Duties of the Sexton:
"All persons buried within the Corporation (Shreveport) shall be interred in the public burying ground (Oakland)." Further, "no pauper shall be buried at the expense of the Corporation except on order of the Mayor, which shall only be granted on proper showing of an oath of sexton or other person."

July 19, 1849: An Ordinance Relating the Burying Ground: "Any person or persons who shall bury or cause to be buried any corpse within the corporation limits of this gown, other than in the public burying ground, shall for each offence pay a fine of not less than $50 and such corpse shall be removed by the Sexton to the burying ground at the expense of the person thus offending."

The ordinance of this date also authorized the survey of the burial ground and created street names for the cemetery: Main Street, Death Street, Rest Street and Peace Street.

"Persons purchasing private burial grounds as family squares shall enclose each square in a manner such as plainly to designate it within 30 days from the purchase thereof, under penalty of a fine of $10 for each week thereafter said square may remain unenclosed."

The mayor was authorized to enclose five acres of the burial ground with "a good and substantial post and rail fence," to keep out horses, cattle and swine.

The ordinance further imposed fines and possible imprisonment of up to twenty-four hours for anyone who "shall deface, disturb, or molest any part of the burying ground; to wit, enclosures, fences, tombs, or tombstones, graves, trees, shrubbery, flowers, or the like."

October 1, 1849: The sexton was authorized "to purchase one shirt, one pair of drawers, one pair of socks, and one pair of gloves worth $3.50 for any pauper who may die in the Town of Shreveport without suitable clothes for funeral purposes."

February 4, 1851: The mayor was authorized to sell to the Society of Odd Fellows, the Freemasons and the Sons of Temperance a block within the burial ground upon them paying fifty dollars in advance to allow them to pay the balance over six, twelve or eighteen months.

The ordinance that had previously authorized the mayor to sell the lots for ten dollars each was amended to read, "Ten dollars in silver or gold" and that any money raised would be reserved to enclose the cemetery.

June 17, 1851: An Ordinance Relating to the Burying Ground:

1. Persons in Shreveport desiring to bury their friends or relatives on the Shreveport Burying Ground or Grave Yard, who do not own lots therein, must apply to the sexton to designate the spot or place of interment and they shall bury the corpse at the spot designated by the sexton.
2. It is the sexton's duty to select the spot of interment and it shall be in the Potter's Field.
3. The sexton shall receive $1.00 for each and every time he shall designate the spot of interment, to be paid by the person or persons applying for the same; and he shall be subject to a fine of $5 for each and every time he fails, refuses, or neglects to designate a burial spot when called on.

4. Any person burying a corpse at any other spot or place than that designated by the sexton shall pay a fine of not less than $25. This shall not apply to persons owning lots in said grave yard. This ordinance shall also not apply to the burial of paupers.
5. All moneys or funds arising from the sales of grave yard lots and from fines imposed for the violation of any ordinance relating to the grave yard shall be set apart as a separate fund to be used for, and expended exclusively for, the improvement of the said grave yard.

January 6, 1853: The mayor stated the city sexton informed him that the road to the grave yard as now used was soon to be closed by the owner of the property through which it runs. He recommended that a road be immediately established and opened to the grave yard.

January 11, 1853: An ordinance to create a street "to commence at Common Street opposite to the west end of Texas Street…to be called Sprague Street."

June 3, 1858: The following ordinance with regard to graveyards enacted on July 19, 1849 (see above) would be published and enforced: "Any person or persons who shall bury or cause to be buried any corpse within the corporate limits of the town, other than the public burying ground, shall for each offense pay a fine of not less than $50.00 and such corpse shall be removed by the sexton to the burying ground at the expense of the person thus offending."

June 7, 1861: An Ordinance:

1. That the laws now existing in relation to the sexton be amended as follows: before burying any person he shall have a certificate signed

by a regular physician, or three respectable citizens, stating the name, age, disease causing the death, and the date of the death, and said certificates to be carefully kept by the sexton and handed in at the close of every month to the clerk of the Board of Health.

2. The sexton failing to comply with the above ordinance shall be fined $50.00 for every offense and confined in the parish jail for 20 days.

March 19, 1863: The sexton's report of deaths for the month of February 1863 reveals eleven deaths in Shreveport, including two cases of "consumption" (tuberculosis), spinal meningitis, scarlet fever and typhus. Six of the deaths were children.

July 3, 1866: A contract was awarded to Collins and Cole for the building of "the grave yard fence and sexton's lodge."

August 16, 1866: The mayor was authorized to employ someone to superintend the burial of paupers during the prevalence of epidemics.

August 3, 1869: An ordinance requiring the city controller to print and provide blank death certificates to practicing physicians in Shreveport: "The city physician will submit them each month at the meeting of the Mayor and Trustees, providing the number of deaths by age."

December 9, 1869: The appointment of a committee to examine the necessity of locating a new graveyard for the city.

July 1, 1873: The sexton was now to be paid five dollars for every grave dug for city paupers.

September 3, 1873: The sum of $500 was appropriated as a charitable fund to employ nurses for the indigent sick of the city. A committee of three members of the city council and the mayor would make arrangements for the Howard Association to have medicinal and other supplies available for the indigent sick population of the city.

September 16, 1873: A specially called meeting of the city council to authorize the mayor to distribute the said funds for the indigent poor.

October 15, 1873: A specially called meeting to authorize the mayor to turn over all funds to the Howard Association on the condition that the organization pay all accounts incurred for the indigent sick with yellow fever at the city hospital.

November 4, 1873: A special resolution of the city council: "Whereas, we have received from all parts of the Union contributions amply sufficient to meet all of our wants and having use for no further donations, therefore be it resolved: that the Mayor is hereby instructed to tender to all those who have so generously come to the assistance of our afflicted people the heartfelt gratitude of the people of Shreveport for their generous acts."

April 21, 1874: The city extended a contract with Dr. J.L. Moore for caring for the indigent sick of the city for 1873, with the contract to continue until Charity Hospital was prepared to receive patients.

June 26, 1875: "Police Officer J.L. Hart, having lost his life on the 13th day of June, 1875, whilst endeavoring to preserve the peace and good order of the city, it is proper that there should not only be a recognition of the sacrifice he made in the discharge of duty, but that his family should be exempt from bearing the expenses attendant upon his death and burial. Therefore, be it resolved that $150.00 be allowed as the salary of said J.L. Hart, deceased, for his services for the month of June 1875 and that a warrant be issued for said sum to Mrs. Hart his surviving widow and tutrix of his minor children and let the funeral costs allowed to be paid."

April 15, 1876: The city council examined charges against George Cumpston, the city sexton, as follows in the majority report: "We, the committee appointed to examine into the charges alleged against George Cumpston, would respectfully report that we regard him as incompetent and having to some extent evidenced neglect of duty; therefore recommend his dismissal. Signed: Thomas Kelly, Administrator of Improvements; Samuel Levy, Administrator of Finance." The minority report: "I do not concur in the report made to the majority of the committee in this case as I am not satisfied that the charges against the city sexton were sustained by sufficient evidence to dismiss him from office. Signed: R. Renfro, Administrator of Accounts."

As a result, a new city sexton, James Butler, was elected. The meeting minutes reflect that Administrator Utz protested the election as a violation of the city charter.

February 1, 1879: The sexton reported that burial room in the paupers' field of the city cemetery was nearly exhausted, whereupon he was given permission to begin burials in the southeast corner of the cemetery.

February 15, 1879: A resolution of the city council addressed taxes assessed against the Hebrew Zion Congregation on lots within the Weinstock Subdivision to be remitted toward the purchase of a cemetery for the Hebrew Zion Congregation.

September 4, 1879: A letter from Mayor Andrew Currie: "I respectfully call the attention of the Council to the burial of paupers in the grave yard. I respectfully call the attention of the Council to the fact that the city sexton has exhausted all ground in the grave yard that could be made available for the burial of paupers, and that some other grounds must be used. The burial of persons by the city authorities under the name of paupers has been greatly abused in the past and the subterfuges now used to get orders for coffins is hard to check, so physicians often endorse the applications. It became very fashionable to be buried as a pauper, the orders obtained being often credited on the price of a stylish coffin, and the dead pauper carried to his grave in the costliest hearse, followed by a string of carriages filled with mourning relatives and friends, and escorted by the benevolent societies of which the person was a member. Paupers are generally defined to be only such indigent persons as are dependent upon the parish or town for maintenance. In order to stop the frequent impositions of this kind, I recommend that the Council contract with whomever furnishes the pauper coffins to take charge of the bodies also, and bury them, and that the city sexton be required to aid the undertaker. This is no less the duty of the city than it is to furnish coffins and graves, very often forsaken, the bodies lying for hours uncared for until the sympathy of some neighbor is aroused, and the authorities appealed to, who can find no body authorized or inclined to take charge unless paid for their trouble; this is particularly the case amongst our colored population. In connection to this matter, I must mention that notice of seizure and sale has been served on the City by the Sheriff, which describes the grounds purchased from Mrs. Alston for a cemetery, pointed out by J.W. Jones to satisfy a judgment in his favor. The bonds issued by the City for the purchase of this ground were declared by the Supreme Court to

	have been illegally issued hence, the consideration is void and ought to remit to revision of title. Some ground near the old packer transferred to the City by His Honor in lieu of taxes could be used for the purpose of a potter's field."
	At this meeting, J.S. Rendall was authorized to furnish coffins for paupers at $1.00 per coffin until January 1, 1880.
September 2, 1880:	Mr. H. Deal, the city sexton, reported to the city council on the scarcity of vacant ground in the cemetery.
February 3, 1882:	The report of the city sexton to the city council shows "an unusual and very heavy mortality during the past year." However, the report "furnishes no data to analyze the cause, and in the absence of any report from the Board of Health, or the officers of Charity Hospital, it is impossible to give you the exact mortality due to the city proper."
	The city sexton also reported that "a new city cemetery is an absolute necessity and a site should be immediately purchased and dedicated. There is hardly any untenanted ground left in our old cemetery, which has been in use ever since our city was founded."
January 4, 1883:	Proposals for furnishing pauper coffins for the coming year were read. J.H. Stoner proposed a bid of $1.50 each; J.S. Rendall proposed a bid of $1.40 each. The contract was again awarded to Rendall.
January 2, 1884:	J.S. Rendall contracted to award pauper coffins for the coming year at a price of $2.25 each.

May 25, 1885: A new contract for city sexton John Murry was read into the record: "The said Murry obligates himself to devote his whole time and work to the said cemetery, making and attending to all burials, disinterments, fixing the streets and walks, draining, cleaning up and improving the grounds in the cemetery, and as an assistant in all such and other work he is to keep with him constantly employed at least one able bodied man and laborer. Further, he obligates himself to keep the fences in good order and repair, the city to furnish all materials such as lumber, posts, nails, etc., and lime to whitewash the premises, and further to do all other work that may seem necessary, in connection with the cemetery which the Council of the City of Shreveport or its proper officers may direct. The said Murry is further to keep a record of all burials and disinterments, to collect all charges and fees for same for the city account and pay over the same to the city comptroller, and further he is to inter the city paupers free of charge."

January 21, 1886: A petition of the Benevolent Association of Confederate Veterans for the donation of Lot 9, Block 11, in the city cemetery was presented and, on motion, granted.

May 13, 1886: M.L. Scovell, chairman of the special committee appointed to examine the condition of the city cemetery, reported that the committee had made a careful examination, found great improvement and recommended the continuation of the contract with the sexton for another year, suggesting also that one of the salaried officials of the city be appointed to visit the cemetery weekly.

March 10, 1887: An electric light was authorized to be placed on the crest of the hill on Sprague Street. The sexton was instructed to take care and close up the step entrance to the cemetery and keep the gates locked at night.

July 14, 1887: A petition by city sexton John Murry to place a small gate entrance to the city cemetery on Sprague Street side was granted.

June 14, 1888: A petition was presented by city sexton John Murry to have the fence around the city cemetery renewed or thoroughly repaired. It was referred to the Committee on Public Buildings and Grounds.

May 14 1890: A letter was read to the mayor and city council from John Murry, city sexton: "I would respectfully call your attention to a matter in connection with the City Cemetery and that is the condition of that part of the cemetery outside of the private lots and used for the burial of paupers, strangers, and the poorer classes of persons who have no lots, and commonly known as potter's field. It is now almost impossible to find room there for a grave, which is very disagreeable and sometimes offensive. But I present this matter to your honorable body from a business standpoint more than from sanitary or other questions that might be involved, and would recommend that a place be provided at least for the burial of the above named class of cases at your earliest convenience. Said cases will comprise over 50% of all burials in the cemetery."

A committee was appointed to report on a solution that would alleviate the situation.

May 14, 1890: A petition was presented and read, signed by the taxpayers and property owners of the fifth ward residing in the neighborhood of the city cemetery, requesting "the removal of Lewd and Kept Women" from the neighborhood. The motion was referred to the city police.

January 22, 1891: "J.S. Rendall will provide paupers' coffins for the coming year at a price of $3.00 each."

March 12, 1891: Bids for grounds for a new city cemetery were opened and read:

"Roland Jones offered 34 acres for $5,500.
"L.S. Crain offered 27 acres for $10,000
"VanHoose and Tomkins offered 40 acres for $11,000.
"Andrew Currie offered 30 acres for $10,500.
"Andrew Currie offered 30 acres for $8,500.
"Andrew Currie offered 60 acres for $17,100."

The bids were referred for discussion at the next meeting.

April 9, 1891: The bids pertaining to the purchase of cemetery grounds opened at the previous meeting were rejected.

May 14, 1891: A petition was read from the Ladies Cemetery Association asking the cooperation of the city council in improving and grading the walks and drives in the city cemetery. The resolution noted in response: "Whereas the Ladies Cemetery Association of our city, holding in dearest memory the ties which bind hearts in bonds of love and affection, and mindful of the dear ones laid at rest in that sacred ground, and whereas they ask the privilege to beautify the city of the dead with flowers, shrubbery, grading, etc. Be it resolved by the City Council in legal assembly, convened that the request be granted and that the streets commissioner be instructed to work the proposed drives in the cemetery under the direction of the above association and that the Hon. Mayor R.T. Vinson and the Committee on Buildings and Grounds give this their special attention."

July 14, 1892: Mr. John Wimbish of the Committee on Buildings and Grounds reported that the fence around the city cemetery was in dilapidated condition and recommended the adoption of the following ordinance: "That the committee be instructed to have a new fence put around the cemetery. The committee was authorized to advertise for sealed bids to be opened at the next meeting."

This meeting once again called for a new city cemetery: "Whereas the last Council failed to act in purchasing a site for a cemetery, and his honor, the Mayor, having recommended action on this matter in his annual message, Resolved that a special committee of three be appointed to select and recommend a suitable site for a cemetery."

July 28, 1892: J.F. Lambert was awarded the bid for putting a new fence around the city cemetery at $295.

August 11, 1892: The special committee appointed on July 14, 1892, to recommend a site for a new cemetery entered a report. The majority recommendation was for "the acquisition of a tract of land containing sixty acres, situated within the corporate limits north of the Catholic cemetery and west of the Fairgrounds and Belt Railway, within 200 yards and parallel to the latter, accessible by said railway and by the Texas plank roadway at all seasons of the year…two thirds of its entire area is covered with a variety of handsome forest trees, which will excite a pleasurable pride of ownership in our citizens, redounding to the credit of your honorable body."

	A minority report of the same committee recommended that "sealed proposals be invited from persons owning lands suitable for the purpose, containing not less than twenty acres."
October 13, 1892:	The previously recorded majority and minority reports were read in city council and the minority position was adopted, with bids to be submitted for a new city cemetery.
February 3, 1893:	W.W.W. Warring was approved to furnish pauper coffins for the coming year at a price of $2.75 each.
March 9, 1893:	Bids for cemetery grounds were opened and read; all propositions were rejected and the committee discharged. A resolution was made that "the ground known as City Park be used as the city cemetery." The city attorney was requested to submit a written opinion on the use of City Park for a cemetery.
April 13, 1893:	On the question as to whether City Park could be used as a cemetery, "it is the opinion of the City Attorney that it can be purposed for this, or for any other public use.' The city controller was authorized to advertise for bids for a new cemetery for not less than twenty acres, with said bids to be opened at the next meeting of the city council.
May 11, 1893:	Four sealed bids for lands for a new city cemetery were opened and read. All four bids were rejected.
June 15, 1893:	"It was moved and passed to accept the property previously offered by VanHoose and Tomkins of 20 acres at $125.00 per acre, payable in five equal annual installments at 6% interest."

September 14, 1893:	A report made to the city council highlights the lack of public record or details for many of the lots within the cemetery, leaving some question as to whether there had been use of the lots. "Be it ordained by the Council of the City of Shreveport in legal assembly convened, that all owners of lots in the cemetery be notified by publication in the official journal of the city for 30 days to clean up and put their lots in thorough repair, and in default of said work being done, the Sexton be hereby ordered to have said cleaning done and file his accounts for said work with the city controller, and in default of payment by said owners, the city controller is instructed to advertise and sell such lots the purchase carrying with it the obligation to preserve and not deface the evidence of any interment previously made on said lots."
November 9, 1893:	The Committee on Building and Grounds reported that, in what was known as Potter's Field in the old cemetery, it was "impossible to dig a grave without exhuming the remains of bodies already buried there."
April 11, 1895:	A petition from the Ladies Cemetery Association: "Whereas, the Shreveport cemetery is in a neglected condition, and at a reasonable expense could be adorned and made an ornament to the city by being placed and kept in thorough repair, which would require constant care and a regular source of revenue, and whereas, many owners of lots are dead or have moved away, and to leave the lots abandoned or uncared for, as well as the Potter's Field, which it is the duty of the city to care for, would mar the beauty of the cemetery as a whole, and whereas, the city has derived all the revenues from the sale of cemetery lots and has expended none of it in beautifying

the cemetery, therefore be it resolved by the Shreveport Ladies Cemetery Association that the City Council be earnestly requested to make a regular appropriation in the budget from year to year of not less than $50 per month, the same to be used and expended for the sole purpose of beautifying and keeping in order the Shreveport City Cemetery."

November 21, 1895: The Finance Committee of the city was instructed to put $300 in the budget to be adopted for the year 1896 for the Ladies Cemetery Association.

July 7, 1898: "City prisoners are to be put to work in the cemetery grounds in order to clean and remove overgrown grass and weeds."

August 4, 1898: The Vicksburg, Shreveport and Pacific Railroad was authorized to lay and operate a track on the north side of Cotton Street between Commerce and Market Streets. Permission was given with the condition that the rail company give to Shreveport twenty-five carloads of gravel for use in the cemeteries: "4 carloads for the Catholic Cemetery, 3 carloads to the Jewish Cemetery, 4 carloads to the old city cemetery [Oakland] and the balance to be used on the new city cemetery [Greenwood]."

February 27, 1902: Frank Kane, the city engineer, proposed the building of a retaining wall of brick, a cement sidewalk and all necessary grading within the cemetery at an estimated cost of $3,274.08. The controller was authorized to advertise and accept bids for the work.

March 13, 1902: An ordinance passed relating to grave desecration: "Be it ordained that the City Council in regular session convened that it shall be unlawful for any person to cut or remove from any cemetery in the city, or from any grave in the city, any flower, shrubs, or other plants or in any way desecrate any grave or any part of any cemetery. Be it further ordained that anyone violating this ordinance shall be fined for each offense not less than $5.00 nor more than $10.00, and on failure to pay this fine the offender may be condemned to work same out on the streets and alleys of the city at a rate of $1.00 per day."

November 16, 1903: A request for a retaining wall "on Cane Street from Sprague Street to Reynolds and on Christian Street for a distance of 150 feet, similar to the one on the Sprague Street side of the old cemetery."

January 26, 1904: A petition entered by the Cemetery Association and passed the city council to address the issue of security at Oakland Cemetery: "In view of the public situation of the old cemetery and the repeated depredations of stock and trespassers, we earnestly request that you will aid us in protecting the cemetery by putting a man in charge, whose duty it shall be to watch over as well as work and thus give the needed protection to this sacred ground." The result was the hiring of an "assistant sexton" at fifty dollars per month.

May 31, 1904: The bid of Rueben McKellar was approved for the building of the previously requested cemetery retaining wall.

October 27, 1904: The salary of the sexton was fixed at seventy dollars per month and an assistant sexton at fifty dollars per month, with one stationed at Oakland and one at Greenwood Cemetery. The sexton was expressly forbidden to accept private work or compensation in connection with his duties as a city employee. City prisoners were again recommended as labor to assist with cemetery work, and there was a recommendation to purchase a mule or horse to assist with moving dirt and removing brush and other litter.

April 11, 1905: An Ordinance Providing Regulations for City Cemeteries:

1. It shall be unlawful for any person to destroy any flowers or other shrubbery or trees within cemeteries.
2. No brick work shall be allowed therein except in the construction of foundations to monuments (followed by specific instructions regarding measurements).
3. No vaults shall be constructed above the ground except that they be of stone.
4. No person decorating or cleaning off graves and lots shall leave trash in the cemetery walks, and shall remove all rubbish which they may have caused.
5. No person shall leave open any of the cemetery gates.
6. No person shall drive any vehicle or ride or lead a horse or any other animal across the cemetery lots or in any other place in said cemeteries except on cemetery streets.
7. Any person who shall violate any of the foregoing provisions shall be fined not less than $1.00 nor more than $10.00 and in default of payment of said fine shall be ordered to work out same on streets and alleys or other public works of the City of Shreveport at the rate of $1.00 per day."

June 23, 1905: The Improvement Committee recommended modifications to the retaining walls on Cane Street extending to Reynolds Street and on Christian Street that would be four feet high with an iron fence on top and a terrace from there to the top of the surface of the ground.

April 17, 1906:	It was resolved that the mayor issue a certificate to Rueben McKellar, contractor, for the sum of $5,973.83, bearing 5 percent interest, in payment of the balance due on the cemetery wall.
June 14, 1906:	The city controller was authorized to sell lots within Oakland Cemetery, specifying lot numbers, "with all lots being within what has heretofore been known as 'A Place for the Friendless.' The prices on the above lots being $100.00."
July 16, 1906:	A dispute recorded in the city council in which Mayor Querbes reported that work done on the Grand Avenue entrance by R.N. McKellar had been without authorization. The mayor suggested that the city council should not pay the account.
August 14, 1906:	McKellar appeared before the city council and presented a claim against the City of Shreveport for work done on the cemetery wall on Cane and Reynolds Streets side, and for ongoing interest accruing on the Christian Street side. McKellar also entered formal claim for payment on the Grand Avenue entrance. Mayor Querbes stated that McKellar was not entitled to the payment for the amount claimed and that the gate at Grand Avenue had been put in without approval.
October 11, 1906:	Communication from McKellar entered into the record requesting that the difference claimed by him on the cemetery wall be submitted to arbitration, with the city to choose an arbitrator and McKellar to choose another and both sides to agree to bind themselves to the decision. The proposition was rejected.
May 14, 1907:	The city council approved the mayor's order that bodies of African Americans buried in the

old cemetery should be disinterred and buried in another cemetery in order to have a straight road built in the graveyard.

August 13, 1907: The city council approved the employment of a special police officer to patrol Oakland Cemetery between dark and daylight and "to see also that the gates of this cemetery be locked from 8 o'clock at night until the officer leaves in the morning, from this time until November 15, or as long thereafter as your Honor may deem necessary."

April 14, 1908: The city council noted that within a year, the city would be without any remaining space in Oakland Cemetery.

Notes

Introduction

1. "Oakland Cemetery Timeline," Shreveport City Council Records, Louisiana State University–Shreveport Noel Memorial Library, Archives and Special Collections, Vertical File (Cemeteries).
2. Jane Newberry, "Oakland Cemetery: Its Trials and Tribulations: The Evolution of a National Historic Landmark." *North Louisiana Historical Association Journal*, 19, no. 2: 3.
3. Bill Bowen, "Here Lies History," *Shreveport Journal*, April 27, 1990, 5-B, Louisiana State University–Shreveport Noel Memorial Library, Archives and Special Collections, Vertical File (Cemeteries).
4. "Oakland Cemetery Timeline."
5. Although the historic marker on the Yellow Fever Mound states 759 dead, this figure comes from the November 15, 1873 tabulation in the *Shreveport Times*. Using the daily tallies between August 20, 1873, and November 12, 1873, 724 bodies were interred within the mound. Additionally, around seventy-five other graves have been identified under marked monuments within the cemetery. Others are very likely as well.
6. Bailey Thomson, "Historic Shreveport," *Shreveport Journal*, 1980, 59.

Alexander John Boarman

7. Arthur W. Bergeron Jr., *Guide to Louisiana Confederate Military Units 1861–1865* (Baton Rouge: Louisiana State University Press, 1989), 72.
8. Maude Hearn O'Pry, *Chronicles of Shreveport* (Shreveport, LA: Journal Publishing Co., 1928), 257.
9. Eric Brock, *Shreveport Chronicles: Profiles from Louisiana's Port City* (Charleston, SC: The History Press, 2009), 41.
10. Ibid., 42.
11. O'Pry, *Chronicles of Shreveport*, 257.

Jacob Bodenheimer

12. Susan Gross, *Wings Toward the South: The First Hundred Years of Congregation Agudath Achim* (Shreveport, LA: Congregation Agudath Achim, 1999), 1.
13. Oakland Cemetery Collection, Noel Archives, Louisiana State University–Shreveport.

Mary Bennett Cane

14. *Shreveport Times*, May 15, 1902.
15. Viola Carruth, *Caddo 1,000: A History of the Shreveport Area from the Time of the Caddo Indians to the 1970s*. (Shreveport, LA: Shreveport Magazine, 1970), 28.
16. *Shreveport Times*, May 15, 1977.
17. Ibid.

Amanda Arnell Clark and Dr. Dickerson Alphonse Smith (Mother and Son)

18. Tenth Decennial Census (1880), untabulated returns for Caddo Parish, Louisiana.
19. *Shreveport Times*, "LSU Still Studying Artifacts Unearthed at Downtown Site," February 18, 1986.
20. Willie Burton, *On the Black Side of History*, (Shreveport, LA, 1994), 53.

Lawrence Pike Crain

21. Lawrence Pike Crain papers, Noel Archives and Special Collections, Louisiana State University–Shreveport.
22. Brock, *Shreveport Chronicles*, 20–21.
23. Ibid.

Moses H. Crowell

24. Tom Ruffin, "When Shreveport Had 3…Count 'Em…Mayors," *Shreveport Magazine*, August 1970, 24.
25. Ibid.

Adah Vinson DeLay

26. O'Pry, *Chronicles of Shreveport*, 345.
27. Ibid.

Bartholomew Egan

28. *Biographical and Historical Memoirs of Northwest Louisiana* (Nashville, TN: Southern Publishing Company, 1890), 162.
29. Ibid.
30. Bartholomew Egan, *Report of the Surgeon General of the State of Louisiana*, 1864, worldcat.org/title/report-of-the-adjutant-general-and-surgeon-general-of-the-state-of-louisiana/oclc/22193736?referer=di&ht=edition.
31. Wilfred Buck Yearns, *The Confederate Governors* (Athens: University of Georgia Press, 1985), 104.
32. Ibid.
33. Seventh decennial U.S. census (1850), untabulated returns for Bienville Parish, Louisiana.

Claiborne Lee Foster

34. George W. Cullum, *Biographical Register of the Officers and Graduates of the United States Military Academy at West Point, New York, Since Its Establishment in 1802* (Cambridge, MA: Riverside Press, 1901), 3:419.
35. Ibid.; ibid., 4:464.
36. Charles Kappler, ed., "Part III—Executive Orders Relating to Indian Reserves (Fort Reno Military Reserve)," *Indian Affairs: Laws and Treaties* (Washington, D.C.: Government Printing Office, 1904) 1:415–19, 842–43.
37. Cullum, *Biographical Register*, 4:464; Bogan-Foster Papers, Louisiana State University–Shreveport Noel Memorial Library, Archives and Special Collections, Vertical File (Cemeteries).
38. Cullum, *Biographical Register*, 4:464; Bogan-Foster Papers, Louisiana State University–Shreveport Noel Memorial Library, Archives and Special Collections, Vertical File (Cemeteries).

Captain James Martin Foster

39. Cullum, *Biographical Register*, 4:464; Bogan-Foster Papers, Louisiana State University–Shreveport Noel Memorial Library, Archives and Special Collections, Vertical File (Cemeteries).
40. James M. Foster, *In Memoriam* (New York: Fleming Revell Company, 1900), 9.
41. *Shreveport Caucasian*, December 12, 1900.
42. Lilla McLure and J. Ed Howe, *History of Shreveport and Shreveport Builders* (Shreveport, LA: J. Ed Howe, 1937), 290.
43. *Shreveport Times*, "Obituary for Captain James Martin Foster," December 12, 1900.

John Gray Foster

44. *New York Times*, June 13, 1901.
45. Ibid.
46. Ibid., June 21, 1901.
47. Bogan-Foster Papers, State of Louisiana, Parish of Bossier Clerk of Court, Warrant and Bill of Indictment of Prince Edwards for the murder of John Gray Foster, Noel Archives, Louisiana State University–Shreveport.
48. *Shreveport Times*, June 21, 1901.

WILLIAM WALTON GEORGE

49. Carruth, *Caddo 1,000*, 8.
50. Ibid.
51. "William Walton George," Ancestry.com (accessed October 1, 2014).
52. *Shreveport Daily News*, August 31, 1861.

NATHAN GOLDKIND

53. Brock, *Shreveport Chronicles*, 184.
54. *State of Louisiana v. Gus Logan* No. 6214; *Supreme Court of Louisiana v. Gus Logan*, 37 LA Ann. 778, No. 165, Governor McEnery's commutation attached to file.

JOHN LEE GOOCH

55. Louisiana State Supreme Court, *Reports of Cases Argued and Determined in the Supreme Court of Louisiana*, vol. 24, 1872 (New Orleans, LA: Republican Office, 1872), 465–67.
56. "Oakland Cemetery Timeline."

JAMES MADISON HOLLINGSWORTH

57. Andrew B. Booth, *Records of Louisiana Confederate Soldiers and Louisiana Confederate Commands* (New Orleans: Commissioner of Louisiana Military Records, 1920), 3:338.
58. McLure and Howe, *History of Shreveport and Shreveport Builders*, 258–60.
59. "Reconstruction: A State Divided," Cabildo, Louisiana State Museum.
60. Joe Gray Taylor, *Louisiana: A History* (Baton Rouge: Louisiana State University Press, 1976), 111.
61. U.S. House of Representatives, *Louisiana Affairs: Report Relating to the Condition of the South* (Washington, D.C: Government Printing Office, 1875), 792.
62. Ted Tunnell, *The Edge of the Sword* (Baton Rouge: Louisiana State University Press, 2001), 190.

THOMAS P. HOTCHKISS

63. Seventh decennial U.S. census (1850), untabulated returns for Caddo Parish, Louisiana.
64. Booth, *Records of Louisiana Confederate Soldiers*, 3:359.
65. Lavender U.S. Soil Survey Map of 1906, Noel Archives, Louisiana State University–Shreveport; Clifton Cardin, *Bossier Parish History: The First 150 Years 1843–1993* (Shreveport, LA, 1993), 62.

JOHN N. HOWELL

66. O'Pry, *Chronicles of Shreveport*, 88.
67. Ibid.
68. *Shreveport Times*, "Down Memory Lane," June 24, 1935.
69. Eric Brock, *Shreveport* (Baton Rouge, LA: Pelican Publishing, 2001), 249.

BENJAMIN JACOBS

70. Benjamin Jacobs's passport application, dated June 22, 1875, to travel to Prussia, Ancestry.com (accessed October 1, 2014).
71. "Benjamin Jacobs," *Louisiana Historical Association*, lahistory.org/site27.php (accessed October 1, 2014).
72. "Presidential Pardon of Benjamin Jacobs," U.S. Government Public Records File, Ancestry.com (accessed October 1, 2014).
73. John Hope Franklin, *Reconstruction After the Civil War* (Chicago: University of Chicago Press, 1961), 34.

EDWARD JACOBS

74. Brock, *Shreveport Chronicles*, 14.
75. General Francis, "An Old Building and Fond Memories," *Shreveport Times*, April 14, 1957.
76. *Biographical and Historical Memoirs*, 74.
77. General Francis, "An Old Building and Fond Memories."

78. Jo Ann Carrigan, *The Saffron Scourge: A History of Yellow Fever in Louisiana, 1796–1905* (Lafayette: Center for Louisiana Studies, University of Southwestern Louisiana, 1994), 109.

ROLAND JONES

79. O'Pry, *Chronicles of Shreveport*, 252–53.
80. U.S. House of Representatives, *History, Art, and Archives*, house.gov (accessed September 15, 2014).
81. The medal is one of only two of the seven believed to exist. It is owned by Rose Randall Patton, a descendant, and is housed in her personal collection.

ISAAC KAHN

82. Booth, *Records of Louisiana Confederate Soldiers*, 3:495.
83. Eric Brock, *The Jewish Community of Shreveport* (Charleston, SC: Arcadia Press, 2002), 17.

WILLIAM KINNEY

84. Obituary of William Kinney, *Confederate Veteran Magazine*, March 1908.
85. Ibid.
86. *Shreveport City Directory*, 1875 issue.
87. Brock, *Shreveport Chronicles*, 129–31.

THOMAS THOMPSON LAND

88. "Thomas Thompson Land," *Biographical and Historical Memoirs*, 101.
89. State of Louisiana, *Official Journal of the Proceedings of the Constitutional Convention of the State of Louisiana held in New Orleans, 21 April 1879.*

90. Ibid.
91. Ibid.

John Morgan Landrum

92. O'Pry, *Chronicles of Shreveport*, 6.
93. *Biographical Directory of the United States Congress* (Washington, D.C.: Government Printing Office, 2014).
94. Brock, *Shreveport*, 90.

Albert Harris Leonard

95. Ibid., 28.
96. Andrew B. Booth, *Records of Louisiana Confederate Soldiers*, 3:730.
97. McLure and Howe, *History of Shreveport and Shreveport Builders*, 294.
98. Ibid.

Captain Simon Levy Jr.

99. Booth, *Records of Louisiana Confederate Soldiers*, 3:746.
100. Brock, *Jewish Community of Shreveport*, 26.
101. Parish of Caddo, "Railroads," *Caddo Parish History*, Caddo.org (accessed October 20, 2014).
102. State of Louisiana, "LSU Health Sciences Center History," lsuhschistory.org (accessed October 20, 2014).
103. "B'nai Zion Temple," *Institute of Southern Jewish Life*, Isjl.org (accessed October 20, 2014).

SAMUEL LEVY

104. Booth, *Records of Louisiana Confederate Soldiers*, 3:746.
105. Goldring/Woldenberg Institute of Southern Jewish Life, "Samuel Levy," retrieved from www.isjl.org (accessed October 20, 2014).
106. Ninth decennial U.S. census (1870), untabulated returns for Caddo Parish, Louisiana; research by the Red River Regional Studies Center at Louisiana State University–Shreveport for the Oakland Cemetery Preservation Society, 2007 to the present.

LAFAYETTE ROBERT LOGAN

107. Lafayette Robert Logan, Findagrave.com, memorial No. 110024205.
108. "Obituary of L.R. Logan," *Shreveport Times*, September 21, 1919.
109. Brock, *Shreveport*, 68.
110. *Shreveport Times*, January 15, 1908.
111. Ibid.
112. Brock, *Shreveport*, 68.

COLONEL LEON DAWSON MARKS

113. Brock, *Shreveport Chronicles*, 31.
114. State of Louisiana, *Official Journal of the Proceedings of the Constitutional Convention of the State of Louisiana held in New Orleans, 21 April 1879.*
115. Booth, *Records of Louisiana Confederate Soldiers*, 3:877; Alan C. Richard and Mary M. Richard, *The Defense of Vicksburg: A Louisiana Chronicle* (College Station: Texas A&M University Press, 2004), 107.

ANNIE MCCUNE

116. Goodloe Stuck, *Annie McCune: Shreveport Madam* (Baton Rouge, LA: Moran Publishers, 1981), 4.
117. Ibid., 7.

118. Twelfth decennial U.S. census, untabulated reports for Caddo Parish, Louisiana, Roll T623_560; Page: 1B; Enumeration District: 39.
119. Stuck, *Annie McCune*, 8.

REUBEN NEIL MCKELLAR

120. *Shreveport Magazine,* October 1923.
121. McLure and Howe, *History of Shreveport and Shreveport Builders*, 318.
122. Ibid.

JAMES V. NOLAN

123. Booth, *Records of Louisiana Confederate Soldiers*, 3:1,290.
124. "James V. Nolan, Caddo Parish, Louisiana," *Biographical and Historical Memoirs*, 88–89.

GENEVIEVE PENICK

125. O'Pry, *Chronicles of Shreveport*, 377.
126. Mary Sharon Thomas, "Genevieve Orphanage: Philosophy Outlives Center's Name," *Shreveport Times*, May 6, 1984.
127. Ibid.

JULIA SPARKE RULE

128. McLure and Howe, *History of Shreveport and Shreveport Builders*, 237.
129. Julia Sparke Rule, Findagrave.com, Memorial No. 36791303.
130. McLure and Howe, *History of Shreveport and Shreveport Builders*, 237.
131. *Shreveport Times*, April 7, 1888.
132. Ibid., April 29, 1931.
133. Ibid., August 23, 1959.

COLONEL WILLIAM RABUN SHIVERS

134. Bergeron, *Guide to Louisiana Confederate Military Units*, 71–72.
135. Carruth, *Caddo 1,000*, 47.
136. "William Rabun Shivers," Ancestry.com.
137. Ruffin, "When Shreveport Had 3," 24.
138. Ibid.
139. "William Rabun Shivers."

RICHARD AND ZACHARY TAYLOR

140. Michael Parrish. *Richard Taylor, Soldier Prince of Dixie* (Raleigh: University of North Carolina Press, 1992), 281.
141. Matthew Raynor and Andrew Cliff, *War Epidemics: Historical Geography of Infectious Diseases in Military Conflict and Civil Strife* (New York: Oxford University Press, 2004), 41.

REVEREND GEORGE TUCKER

142. W.E. Paxton, *A History of the Baptists of Louisiana* (St. Louis, MO: C.R. Barns Publishing Company, 1888), 561.
143. Ibid., 562.
144. *Biographical and Historical Memoirs*, 22.
145. William Henry King, *No Pardons to Ask nor Apologies to Make* (Knoxville: University of Tennessee Press, 2006), 124–25.

RICHARD TUCKER VINSON

146. O'Pry, *Chronicles of Shreveport*, 185.
147. Booth, *Records of Louisiana Confederate Soldiers*, 3:940.
148. "Capt. R.T. Vinson, Caddo Parish, Louisiana," *Biographical and Historical Memoirs*, 103.
149. O'Pry, *Chronicles of Shreveport*, 187.

COLONEL SAMUEL J. WARD

150. Samuel J. Ward, Findagrave.com, No. 11.
151. Ibid.
152. McLure and Howe, *History of Shreveport and Shreveport Builders*, 243.
153. Garnie William McGinty, *A History of Louisiana* (n.p.: Exposition Press, 1949), 214–19.
154. Ibid.

LIEUTENANT EUGENE AUGUSTUS WOODRUFF

155. Eugene and George Woodruff Collection (1881), Louisiana State University–Shreveport Noel Memorial Library, Archives and Special Collections, Vertical File (Cemeteries).
156. "History of Buchanan, Iowa," Eugene and George Woodruff Collection (1881), Louisiana State University–Shreveport Noel Memorial Library, Archives and Special Collections, Vertical File (Cemeteries).
157. *Shreveport Times*, October 31, 1929.
158. City of Shreveport Resolution, November 3, 1873, Eugene and George Woodruff Collection (1881), Louisiana State University–Shreveport Noel Memorial Library, Archives and Special Collections, Vertical File (Cemeteries).

YELLOW FEVER MOUND

159. Holy Trinity Catholic Church, "Yellow Fever Epidemic of 1873," http://www.holytrinity-shreveport.com (accessed April 6, 2010).
160. "Report of the Committee on the Yellow Fever Epidemic of 1873 of Shreveport, Louisiana," *American Journal of the Medical Sciences* 66, no. 134 (April 1874), 480–82; *Shreveport Times*, August 24, 1873; Panorama photograph by the U.S. Army Corps of Engineers, August 20, 1873, Louisiana State University–Shreveport Noel Memorial Library, Archives and Special Collections, Vertical File (Cemeteries).
161. "Report of the Committee on the Yellow Fever Epidemic of 1873."
162. Ibid.

163. Jo Ann Carrigan, "Impact of Epidemic Yellow Fever on Life in Louisiana," *Louisiana History: The Journal of the Louisiana Historical Association* 4, no. 1 (Winter 1963), 5.
164. World Health Organization, http://www.who.int.
165. "Yellow Fever," Department of Health and Human Services, Centers for Disease Control and Prevention, http://www.cdc.gov (accessed April 6, 2010).
166. Eugene and George Woodruff Collection, (1881).
167. *New York Times*, "How Burials Are Made in Shreveport—The Disease Imported From Cuba and Appeal to the People," September 30, 1873.
168. Ibid.
169. *Shreveport Times*, November 15, 1873.
170. Ibid.
171. Research by the Red River Regional Studies Center at Louisiana State University–Shreveport for the Oakland Cemetery Preservation Society, 2007 to the present.
172. L. Hanggi-Myers, "The Howard Association of New Orleans—Precursor to District Nursing," *Public Health Nursing*, 12, no. 2 (1995), 78–82.
173. E.Y. Newsom, "Unto the Least of These: The Howard Association and Yellow Fever," *South Medical Journal* 856, no. 6 (June 1992), 632–37.
174. "Report of the Committee on the Yellow Fever Epidemic of 1873 of Shreveport, Louisiana." Further research indicates that the first case was probably noted on August 20, 1873, but was misdiagnosed. The last reported case was diagnosed on November 12, 1873.

About the Authors

Gary D. Joiner, PhD

Gary D. Joiner, PhD, received a bachelor of arts in history and geography from Louisiana Tech University, a master of arts in history from Louisiana Tech University and a doctorate in history from St. Martin's College, Lancaster University in the United Kingdom. He is a professor of history at Louisiana State University in Shreveport and serves as the chair of the Department of History and Social Sciences, where he holds the Mary Anne and Leonard Selber Professorship in History and serves as the director of the Red River Regional Studies Center. He is the author or editor of twenty-one books, including *History Matters, Shiloh and the Western Campaign of 1862*; *One Damn Blunder from Beginning to End, Through the Howling Wilderness*; *The Red River Campaign: The Union's Last Attempt to Invade Texas*; *No Pardons to Ask nor Apologies to Make*; *Little to Eat and Thin Mud to Drink*; *Mr. Lincoln's Brown Water Navy*; *Red River Steamboats*; *Historic Shreveport-Bossier*; *Lost Shreveport: Vanishing Scenes from the Red River Valley*; *Historic Haunts of Shreveport*; and *Wicked Shreveport*. Dr. Joiner is also the author of numerous articles and technical reports, and he has served as a consultant for ABC, the Associated Press, A&E Network, C-SPAN, the Discovery Network, HGTV, the History Channel, MSNBC, MTV and the SyFy Channel, among others.

Cheryl H. White, PhD

Cheryl H. White, PhD, is an assistant professor of history at Louisiana State University at Shreveport and has coauthored two other books with The History Press: *Historic Haunts of Shreveport* and *Wicked Shreveport*. In addition, she is the author of *Confederate General Leonidas Polk: Louisiana's Fighting Bishop*, published by The History Press in 2013, and has another forthcoming title in 2015: *The History and Haunts of Louisiana's Antebellum Plantations*. Dr. White is also the author of numerous articles and encyclopedia entries and has served as a national research consultant. She is the recipient of numerous teaching awards and is actively involved in expanding community interest in the discipline of history through the founding and facilitation of adult library-based reading groups, frequent community lecture series and leading historic preservation tours as fundraisers for some of Shreveport's most endangered sites, including Oakland Cemetery. She also serves on the board of directors of the Oakland Cemetery Preservation Society.